101 Signals From Pet Heaven

Signs your Beloved Pet
Thinks of You in the Afterlife

✓ 101 Veritable Signs that
Your Pet Misses You
✓ Purpose, Guidance, and Meditation
✓ Peace of Mind and Serene Disposition
✓ Visualizations, and Gratitude
✓ Mindset Calibration and Healing
✓ Moving On BUT Never Forgetting
✓ and a Love Letter from Pet Heaven

JUPITERION OLYMPUS © 2023

Disclaimer

The information contained is intended for educational and entertainment purposes only. This book is not intended to be a substitute for professional advice, diagnosis, or treatment. The author and publisher make no representations or warranties with respect to the accuracy or completeness of the contents of this book and specifically disclaim any implied warranties of merchantability or fitness for a particular purpose.

The information contained in this book is presented in good faith and believed to be accurate, but the author and publisher make no representations or warranties as to the accuracy or completeness of the information.

The techniques, tips, and information contained within this book are not intended to diagnose, treat, cure, or prevent any health or financial problems, or psychological disorders.

The reader should always seek the advice of a qualified healthcare professional before starting any new health or wellness program.

The author and publisher shall not be held responsible for any loss, damage, or injury arising from the use of the information contained in this book.

Table of Contents

JUPITERION
www.jupiterion.com

Signal 11

Signal 12

Signal 13

Signal 14

Signal 15

Signal 16

Signal 17

Signal 18

Signal 19

Signal 20

Signal 21

Signal 22

Signal 23

Signal 24

Signal 25

Signal 26

Signal 27

Signal 28

Signal 29

Signal 30

Signal 31

Signal 32

Signal 33

Signal 34

Signal 35

Signal 36

Signal 37

Signal 38

Signal 39

Signal 40

Signal 41

Signal 42

Signal 43

Signal 44

Signal 45

Signal 46

Signal 47

Signal 48

Signal 49

Signal 50

Signal 51

Signal 52

Signal 53

Signal 54

Signal 55

Signal 56

Signal 57

Signal 58

Signal 59

Signal 60

Signal 61

Signal 62

Signal 63

Signal 64

Signal 65

Signal 66

Signal 67

Signal 68

Signal 69

Signal 70

Signal 71

Signal 72

Signal 73

Signal 74

Signal 75

Signal 76

Signal 77

Signal 78

Signal 79

Signal 80

Signal 81

Signal 82

Signal 83

Signal 83

Signal 84

Signal 85

Signal 86

Signal 87

Signal 88

Signal 89

Signal 90

Signal 91

Signal 92

Signal 93

Introduction

JUPITERION
www.jupiterion.com

Losing a pet can be one of the most heartbreaking and difficult experiences that we face in life. The bond that we share with our furry companions is one that is built on Trust, Loyalty, and Unconditional Love.

When they pass away, we are left with a hole in our hearts that can seem impossible to fill.

In this deeply empathetic guide, we explore 101 Top Signs that our beloved pets may be communicating with us from beyond the veil.

Through the lens of the afterlife, we offer a glimmer of Hope and Solace for those who are Grieving the Loss of their Furry Family Member.

Whether it's:

- Feeling a Sudden Change in Temperature

- Hearing the Jingle of their Collar
- or Seeing a Vision of their Spirit

and more, these signs can help provide comfort and closure in a time of great sorrow. With each message, we aim to help you reconnect with the memories and the love that you shared with your pet, and to remind you that they will always be with you in spirit.

More than just a guidebook, this is a celebration of the love that we share with our furry family members, and a testament to the resilience of the human spirit.

We hope that the signs in this book will provide a beacon of hope for those who are struggling to move on from the death of their pet, and a reminder that our pets are always with us, watching over us, and forever in our hearts.

Does Your Pet Still Remember You?

Would you know my name...

If I saw you in heaven?

Would it be the same...

If I saw you in heaven?

Those are the immortal words of Eric Clapton from his song about loss entitled Tears In Heaven. Yes, they still know you and still think about you and they show these by sending signs from time to time.

Whenever you miss your pet most especially when you're by your lonesome before you sleep at night, recall the events that happened in your day and look for these 101 signals and you'll know that you're not alone.

You're remembered, appreciated, and unconditionally loved by your beloved pet.

Without further ado, let's start with the first signal.

Signal 1

Hearing your pet's bark, meow, or other vocalizations is a sign that they may be communicating with you from beyond the veil.

This can be an incredibly powerful and emotional experience, as it provides a sense of connection and comfort with your beloved pet.

For example, you may hear your pet's bark or meow coming from a specific location in your home, even though your pet is no longer physically present.

This can be a reminder that your pet is still with you in spirit, watching over you and providing you with love and support from heaven.

In some cases, you may hear your pet's vocalizations when you are feeling particularly sad or upset.

This can be a sign that your pet is trying to

comfort you and provide you with the emotional support that you need during this difficult time.

Another example might be hearing a specific sound or phrase that was unique to your pet.

For example, you might hear the sound of your dog's collar jingling, or the sound of your cat's purring.

These sounds can be a powerful reminder of the bond that you shared with your pet, and can bring up feelings of love and connection.

If you hear your pet's bark, meow, or other vocalization, take a moment to reflect on the emotions and the message that it conveys.

What message may your pet be trying to convey?

How can this experience provide you with comfort and guidance in your life?

Remember that your pet is still with you in spirit, providing you with love and support from beyond the veil.

Hearing their vocalizations is a reminder that their love and their presence will continue to be a part of your life, even after they have passed away.

Signal 2

Seeing your pet's spirit or physical form is a sign that they may be communicating with you from heaven. This can be a profound and emotional experience, providing a sense of comfort and connection with your beloved pet.

For example, you may see a fleeting glimpse of your pet's physical form out of the corner of your eye, even though they are no longer present in the physical world.

You may also see your pet's image in a dream or vision, or feel their presence in the room with you.

In some cases, you may even see your pet's spirit directly, such as a light or mist that takes the shape of your pet.

This can be an incredibly powerful experience, as it provides a direct connection with your pet's spirit and can bring up feelings of love and connection.

If you see your pet's spirit or physical form, take a moment to be present with your emotions and to reflect on the message that it conveys.

What message may your pet be trying to convey?

How can this experience provide you with comfort and guidance in your life?

Above all, seeing your pet's spirit or physical form is a reminder of the deep and unbreakable bond that you shared with your furry family member.

Even after they have left this world, their love and their presence will continue to be a source of comfort and joy in your life.

Signal 3

Feeling your pet's presence is a sign that they may be communicating with you from beyond the veil. This can be an incredibly powerful and emotional experience, providing a sense of comfort and connection with your beloved pet.

For example, you may feel a sense of warmth or a comforting presence in the room, even though your pet is no longer physically present.

This can be a reminder that your pet is still with you in spirit, watching over you and providing you with love and support from heaven.

In some cases, you may also feel a sense of your pet's personality or energy, such as feeling their playful spirit or their calm and nurturing presence.

This can be a reminder of the unique bond that you shared with your pet and can bring up feelings of love and connection.

If you feel your pet's presence, take a moment to be present with your emotions and to reflect on the message that it conveys.

What message may your pet be trying to convey?

How can this experience provide you with comfort and guidance in your life?

Remember that your pet is still with you in spirit, providing you with love and support from beyond the veil. Feeling their presence is a reminder that their love and their presence will continue to be a part of your life, even after they have passed away.

Signal 4

When our pets appear in our dreams, it can be a sign that they are communicating with us from heaven. These dreams can feel incredibly real and may provide a sense of comfort, connection, and guidance as we navigate through the grief and loss of losing our furry family members.

For example, in a dream, your pet may appear healthy, happy, and playing like they used to do when they were alive.

They may also appear to comfort you and show you that they are still with you and watching over you.

Such dreams can be incredibly healing and can provide a sense of closure and comfort in the midst of grief.

In some cases, the dream may be more symbolic or metaphoric, such as seeing your pet running free in an open field or appearing in a bright light.

These dreams can be a reminder that your pet has crossed over into a peaceful and loving realm, where they are free from any pain or suffering.

If your pet appears in your dreams, take a moment to reflect on the emotions and the message that it conveys.

What message may your pet be trying to convey?

How can this experience provide you with comfort and guidance in your life?

Above all, the appearance of your pet in your dreams is a reminder of the deep and unbreakable bond that you shared with your furry family member.

Even after they have left this world, their love and their presence will continue to be a source of comfort and joy in your life.

Signal 5

Smelling your pet's scent is a sign that they may be communicating with you from beyond the veil. This can be a powerful and emotional experience, providing a sense of comfort and connection with your beloved pet.

For example, you may catch a whiff of your pet's scent in a room, even though your pet is no longer physically present.

This can be a reminder that your pet is still with you in spirit, watching over you and providing you with love and support from heaven.

In some cases, you may smell your pet's scent when you are feeling particularly sad or upset.

This can be a sign that your pet is trying to comfort you and provide you with the emotional support that you need during this difficult time.

Another example might be smelling a specific

scent that was unique to your pet, such as their shampoo or the fragrance of their fur.

These scents can be a powerful reminder of the bond that you shared with your pet, and can bring up feelings of love and connection.

If you smell your pet's scent, take a moment to reflect on the emotions and the message that it conveys.

What message may your pet be trying to convey?

How can this experience provide you with comfort and guidance in your life?

Remember that your pet is still with you in spirit, providing you with love and support from beyond the veil. Smelling their scent is a reminder that their love and their presence will continue to be a part of your life, even after they have passed away.

Signal 6

Hearing the sound of your pet's collar jingle can be a profound and emotional experience that may indicate a connection with your beloved pet beyond the physical world.

This experience is one of the many ways that pets can communicate with their owners from beyond the veil, offering comfort and reassurance during a time of grief and loss.

The sound of your pet's collar jingling may appear unexpectedly, and can bring up feelings of nostalgia and longing. It can also be a powerful reminder of the bond that you shared with your pet, and of the joyful moments that you spent together.

For some, hearing the sound of their pet's collar jingle can feel like a sign that their pet is still with them in spirit, watching over them and providing them with love and support.

The sound may appear at moments of heightened emotion or stress, offering a sense of comfort and connection when it is needed most.

It is important to approach these experiences with an open heart and an open mind, as the signs and messages that pets may send from beyond the veil can take many different forms.

By listening to your intuition and allowing yourself to feel your emotions, you may gain a deeper understanding of the ways in which your pet is still present in your life.

Above all, the sound of your pet's collar jingling is a reminder of the deep and unbreakable bond that you shared with your furry family member. Even after they have passed away, their love and their presence will continue to be a source of comfort and joy in your life.

So, if you hear the sound of your pet's collar jingle, take a moment to reflect on the emotions and the message that it conveys. What message may your pet be trying to communicate?

How can this experience provide you with comfort and guidance in your life?

Remember that your pet is still with you in

spirit, providing you with love and support from beyond the veil.

Signal 7

Finding feathers or other objects in unusual places can be a powerful sign that your beloved pet is communicating with you from beyond the physical world.

These experiences can be unexpected and emotional, providing a sense of comfort and connection with your furry family member.

For example, you may find a feather in your home or in a location where your pet is no longer physically present.

This can be a reminder that your pet is still with you in spirit, watching over you and providing you with love and support from heaven.

Other objects, such as toys or treats, may also appear unexpectedly, offering a sense of connection and reassurance during a time of grief and loss.

It is important to approach these experiences with an open heart and an open mind, as the signs and messages that pets may send from beyond the veil can take many different forms.

By listening to your intuition and allowing yourself to feel your emotions, you may gain a deeper understanding of the ways in which your pet is still present in your life.

Above all, finding feathers or other objects in unusual places is a reminder of the deep and unbreakable bond that you shared with your furry family member.

Even after they have passed away, their love and their presence will continue to be a source of comfort and joy in your life.

If you experience these signs, take a moment to reflect on the emotions and the message that they may convey.

What message may your pet be trying to communicate?

How can these experiences provide you with comfort and guidance in your life?

Remember that your pet is still with you in

spirit, providing you with love and support from beyond the veil.

Signal 8

Seeing rainbows or other signs of light can be a powerful and emotional experience that may signify a connection with your pet beyond the physical realm.

These signs can appear in unexpected moments, such as when you are feeling particularly sad or upset, and can serve as a gentle reminder that your pet is still with you in spirit.

Rainbows, in particular, are often associated with hope, renewal, and the promise of a brighter future.

For some, seeing a rainbow after the loss of a pet can be a sign that their furry family member is still present in their lives, providing them with love and support from beyond the veil.

Other signs of light may also appear unexpectedly, such as a bright flash of light or a sudden beam of sunlight.

These signs can be powerful reminders of the bond that you shared with your pet and of the joyful moments that you spent together.

It is important to approach these experiences with an open heart and an open mind, as the signs and messages that pets may send from beyond the veil can take many different forms.

By listening to your intuition and allowing yourself to feel your emotions, you may gain a deeper understanding of the ways in which your pet is still present in your life.

Above all, seeing rainbows or other signs of light is a reminder of the deep and unbreakable bond that you shared with your furry family member.

Even after they have passed away, their love and their presence will continue to be a source of comfort and joy in your life.

Signal 9

Feeling a sudden change in temperature can be a powerful and unexplainable experience that can provide a sense of connection to a beloved pet that has passed away.

These experiences may come as a sudden chill or warmth that cannot be explained by any external factors.

For some people, this sudden shift in temperature can feel like a direct message from their pet, a way of reminding them of the deep and unbreakable bond they shared during their time together.

This experience can be profound and emotional, providing a sense of comfort and connection during times of grief and loss.

It is important to approach these experiences with an open heart and an open mind, as the signs and messages that pets may send from beyond the physical realm can take many different forms.

By listening to your intuition and allowing yourself to feel your emotions, you may gain a deeper understanding of the ways in which your pet is still present in your life.

Above all, feeling a sudden change in temperature is a reminder of the love and connection that we share with our pets, and the lasting impact they can have on our lives.

Whether it is a sudden chill on a warm day or a warm feeling on a cold day, these experiences can be a sign that our pets are still with us, providing comfort and love from beyond the physical realm.

For example, one person may feel a sudden and unexplainable warmth on their chest during a moment of deep sadness, reminding them of their pet's love and presence.

Another person may experience a sudden chill in a room, and feel a sense of peace and comfort knowing that their pet is still with them in spirit.

These experiences are unique to each individual, but they can provide a powerful sense of connection to the pets we love and miss.

Signal 10

When a pet passes away, their absence can feel overwhelming, leaving a void that can be difficult to fill. However, it is not uncommon for people to report experiencing a deep sense of connection and comfort when their pet appears in photographs or videos.

These experiences can be unexpected, and often come as a surprise when people discover their pet's image in a photograph they did not expect.

This can be a sign that their pet is still with them in spirit, and that their love and presence continue to provide a source of comfort and support.

For some, these experiences may be accompanied by a sense of peace and reassurance, as if their pet is telling them that they are still present in their life.

For others, seeing their pet in a photograph or video may bring back memories and a sense of the bond that they shared, providing a source of comfort and healing.

It is important to approach these experiences with an open heart and an open mind, as the signs and messages that pets may send from beyond the veil can take many different forms.

By listening to your intuition and allowing yourself to feel your emotions, you may gain a deeper understanding of the ways in which your pet is still present in your life.

Above all, seeing your pet in photographs or videos is a reminder of the deep and unbreakable bond that you shared with your furry family member.

Even after they have passed away, their love and their presence will continue to be a source of comfort and joy in your life.

For example, one person may discover their pet's image in an old photograph they had forgotten about, bringing back memories and a sense of connection to their pet.

Another person may see their pet's image in

a video that they were watching for the first time, providing them with a sense of peace and reassurance during a difficult time.

These experiences are unique and personal, but they can provide a powerful reminder of the love and connection that we share with our pets.

Signal 11

If you have lost a beloved pet, seeing their favorite toy or object can be an incredibly emotional experience. These items hold special memories and can bring to mind the joy and love that your pet brought into your life.

Whether you come across them unexpectedly or actively seek them out, these objects can serve as a powerful reminder of your pet's presence in your life.

When you see your pet's favorite toy or object, it can feel like a sign that they are still with you in spirit.

It can provide a sense of comfort and reassurance that your pet's love and bond with you is still strong and enduring, even beyond the physical realm.

It is important to approach these experiences with an open heart and an open mind, as the signs and messages that pets may send from beyond the veil can take many different forms.

By listening to your intuition and allowing yourself to feel your emotions, you may gain a deeper understanding of the ways in which your pet is still present in your life.

Above all, seeing your pet's favorite toy or object is a reminder of the deep and unbreakable bond that you shared with your furry family member.

Even after they have passed away, their love and their presence will continue to be a source of comfort and joy in your life.

For example, you may find your pet's favorite ball or toy tucked away in a closet or drawer, and holding it may bring back memories of playing together and the joy it brought to both you and your pet.

Seeing their favorite object can be a powerful way of connecting with your pet's spirit and finding comfort in their continued presence in your life.

Signal 12

When you come across your pet's paw prints, it can be an emotional and heartwarming experience. These prints serve as a beautiful reminder of the love and bond that you shared with your furry companion, and can provide a sense of comfort and connection during times of grief and loss.

Paw prints can take many different forms, from impressions left in the sand or dirt to ink prints taken at the vet's office.

These prints can evoke memories of playful moments, quiet snuggles, and the joy and love that your pet brought into your life.

Seeing your pet's paw prints can feel like a direct message from your pet, a sign that they are still with you in spirit, and a reminder that your love for each other endures beyond physical boundaries.

It is important to approach these experiences with an open heart and an open mind, as the signs and messages that pets may send from beyond the veil can take many different forms.

By listening to your intuition and allowing yourself to feel your emotions, you may gain a deeper understanding of the ways in which your pet is still present in your life.

Above all, seeing your pet's paw prints is a reminder of the deep and unbreakable bond that you shared with your furry family member.

Even after they have passed away, their love and their presence will continue to be a source of comfort and joy in your life.

For example, you may find your pet's paw prints in the sand on a beach that you visited together, bringing back memories of the joy and playfulness that you shared.

Alternatively, you may discover an old ink print that you took at the vet's office, reminding you of the bond that you shared and the love that your pet had for you.

Whatever the form of the paw prints you encounter, they can provide a powerful connection to your pet's spirit and a source of comfort in times of grief and loss.

Signal 13

Feeling your pet brush up against you can be a sign that they are still with you in spirit, and a reminder that your bond with them is unbreakable.

It can bring comfort and reassurance during times of grief and loss, and can serve as a powerful reminder of the love and joy that your pet brought into your life.

When you feel your pet brush up against you, it can be a powerful and emotional moment. It can feel like a direct message from your pet, a sign that they are still with you and that the bond you shared is still strong and enduring.

It is important to approach these experiences with an open heart and an open mind, as the signs and messages that pets may send from beyond the veil can take many different forms.

By listening to your intuition and allowing

yourself to feel your emotions, you may gain a deeper understanding of the ways in which your pet is still present in your life.

Above all, feeling your pet brush up against you is a reminder of the deep and unbreakable bond that you shared with your furry family member.

Even after they have passed away, their love and their presence will continue to be a source of comfort and joy in your life.

For example, you may be sitting on the couch watching television and feel a gentle brush against your leg.

You may turn to look, expecting to see your pet, but find that they are not there. This can be a powerful moment, reminding you of the bond that you shared and the love that your pet had for you.

Alternatively, you may be going about your day and suddenly feel a gentle nudge against your hand, as if your pet is still there, by your side.

These moments can be incredibly emotional and can serve as a powerful reminder that your pet's love and presence are still with you, even beyond the physical realm.

Signal 14

Hearing your pet's name being called can be a powerful sign that your pet is still with you in spirit.

This sign can feel like a direct message from your pet, a reminder that the bond you shared continues beyond the physical realm. It can bring a sense of comfort and reassurance during times of grief and loss, and can remind you of the love and joy that your pet brought into your life.

When you hear your pet's name being called, it can be a poignant reminder of the unique bond that you shared with your furry family member.

It can also serve as a powerful message that your pet is still with you in spirit and that the love you shared continues to endure.

It is important to approach these experiences with an open heart and an open mind, as the signs and messages that pets may send from beyond the veil can take many different forms.

For example, you may be walking down the street and overhear someone calling out your pet's name.

Alternatively, you may be going about your day and suddenly have a vivid memory of your pet's name come to mind.

These moments can be powerful and emotional, reminding you of the love and joy that your pet brought into your life and serving as a source of comfort during times of grief and loss.

Signal 15

Seeing a vision of your pet can be a profound and emotional experience, bringing comfort and reassurance during times of grief and loss. This sign can take many different forms, from a vivid dream to a waking vision of your pet's physical form.

When you see a vision of your pet, it can feel like a direct message from them, a reminder that they are still with you in spirit and that the bond you shared continues to endure. It can also serve as a powerful message of love and support, helping you to navigate the difficult emotions that often accompany the loss of a furry family member.

By listening to your intuition and allowing yourself to feel your emotions, you may gain a deeper understanding of the ways in which your pet is still present in your life.

For example, you may have a vivid dream

in which your pet appears, bringing a sense of comfort and reassurance.

Alternatively, you may be going about your day and suddenly see a vision of your pet's physical form, as if they are standing right in front of you.

These moments can be incredibly emotional and can serve as a powerful reminder of the love and joy that your pet brought into your life.

In some cases, a vision of your pet may be fleeting, while in others it may be more sustained.

Regardless of the form it takes, this sign can be a powerful and emotional experience, helping you to connect with the love and support of your furry family member, even after they have passed beyond the physical realm.

Signal 16

Feeling your pet's fur or whiskers can be a powerful and emotional sign that your furry family member is still with you in spirit. This sign can take many different forms, from a sudden feeling of their soft fur brushing against your skin to the sensation of their whiskers tickling your cheek.

When you feel your pet's fur or whiskers, it can feel like a direct message from them, a reminder that the bond you shared continues to endure beyond the physical realm.

It is important to approach these experiences with an open heart and an open mind, as the signs and messages that pets may send from beyond the veil can take many different forms.

For example, you may be sitting quietly and suddenly feel a soft brush against your leg, as if your pet is still there by your side.

Alternatively, you may be going about your day and suddenly feel the sensation of your pet's whiskers against your cheek.

These moments can be incredibly emotional and can serve as a powerful reminder of the love and connection that you shared with your furry family member.

Signal 17

When a pet passes away, it is common for their spirit to take on the form of another animal as a way of reaching out to their human family members. This can take many different forms, such as seeing a bird that resembles your pet or a stray cat that bears a striking resemblance to your furry family member.

When your pet appears in the form of another animal, it can feel like a direct message from them, a reminder that their spirit is still with you and that the bond you shared continues to endure

By listening to your intuition and allowing yourself to feel your emotions, you may gain a deeper understanding of the ways in which your pet is still present in your life.

For example, you may be sitting in your backyard and suddenly see a bird perched on a nearby branch that reminds you of your pet's distinctive features.

Alternatively, you may be walking down the street and come across a stray cat that bears a striking resemblance to your furry family member.

These moments can be incredibly emotional and can serve as a powerful reminder of the love and joy that your pet brought into your life.

Signal 18

When a beloved pet passes away, it can be difficult to cope with the feelings of loss and grief. However, one of the many ways that our pets may choose to reach out to us from beyond the veil is by leaving signs that they are still with us. One such sign may be the sudden appearance of your pet's favorite treat or food.

Seeing your pet's favorite treat or food can feel like a direct message from them, reminding you of the joy and love that they brought into your life.

It is important to approach these experiences with an open heart and an open mind, as the signs and messages that pets may send from beyond the veil can take many different forms.

For example, you may be going about your day and suddenly see a bag of your pet's favorite treats in a place where it should not be.

Alternatively, you may open your cupboard

and find a can of your pet's favorite food that you forgot you had.

These moments can be incredibly emotional and can serve as a powerful reminder of the love and joy that your pet brought into your life.

No matter the form it takes, the appearance of your pet's favorite treat or food can be a profound and comforting experience, reminding you that the bond you shared with your furry family member continues to endure beyond the physical realm.

Signal 19

One of the many ways that our pets may choose to reach out to us from beyond the veil is by sending us signs in the form of other animals.

When we see a bird or other animal that reminds us of our beloved pet, it can be a powerful and emotional experience that can help us feel connected to them even after they have passed on.

These signs may take many different forms, such as a bird with distinctive markings or a squirrel with a similar personality to your pet.

They may appear unexpectedly or at times when you are feeling particularly emotional, serving as a comforting reminder of the bond you shared with your furry family member.

By listening to your intuition and allowing yourself to feel your emotions, you may gain a deeper understanding of the ways in which your pet is still present in your life.

For example, you may be walking in the park and suddenly see a bird with distinctive markings that remind you of your pet's fur. Alternatively, you may spot a squirrel with a similar personality to your furry family member.

These moments can be incredibly emotional and can serve as a powerful reminder of the love and joy that your pet brought into your life.

.

Signal 20

Feeling a sudden gust of wind can be a poignant reminder that our pets are still with us in spirit, watching over us from heaven.

While it may seem like a simple and natural occurrence, it can also serve as a sign that our beloved pets are sending us messages from beyond, providing us with comfort and reassurance even after they have crossed over.

These signs may take many different forms, such as a sudden gust of wind on a still day or a sudden rustling of leaves.

They may appear unexpectedly or at times when we are feeling particularly emotional, serving as a gentle reminder that our pets are never truly gone and that their love and spirit remain with us always.

It is important to approach these experiences with an open heart and an open mind, allowing ourselves to feel the emotions that come with the loss of a beloved pet.

For example, you may be sitting in your yard or taking a walk, feeling the warm sun on your face when suddenly a strong gust of wind brushes past you, bringing with it the memory of your pet's presence.

These moments can be incredibly emotional, but they can also serve as a reminder of the deep and unbreakable bond that we share with our furry family members, even after they have crossed over into heaven.

Signal 21

Hearing your pet's favorite song or music can be a heartwarming and unexpected reminder of the special bond you shared with your furry family member.

While it may seem like a coincidence or a small moment, it can also serve as a powerful sign that your pet is still with you in spirit, sending you messages of love and support from beyond.

These signs can take many different forms, such as hearing your pet's favorite song on the radio or a melody that reminds you of your time together.

They may come at unexpected moments or during times when you are feeling particularly emotional, serving as a comforting reminder of the love that you shared with your beloved pet.

By tuning into the signs and messages that your pet may be sending you, you may gain a deeper understanding of the ways in which they continue to be present in your life.

For example, you may be driving in your car, feeling lost in thought when suddenly your pet's favorite song comes on the radio.

The familiarity of the tune and the memories it brings with it can be incredibly emotional, but it can also serve as a gentle reminder that your pet is still with you, providing comfort and support even from heaven.

In moments like these, it is important to take a deep breath, allow yourself to feel the emotions that come with the loss of your pet, and to remember the love and joy that you shared together.

These moments can be difficult, but they can also serve as a powerful reminder of the unbreakable bond that exists between pets and their owners, even after they have passed on.

Signal 22

Feeling a sudden change in air pressure can be a subtle yet powerful reminder of the presence of our pets in our lives, even after they have passed on.

While it may seem like a small and insignificant moment, it can also serve as a sign from our furry family members that they are still with us in spirit, watching over us from heaven.

These signs can take many different forms, such as a sudden drop in air pressure, a cool breeze on a warm day, or a warm gust of wind on a cold day.

They may come at unexpected moments or during times when we are feeling particularly emotional, serving as a comforting reminder of the love and connection that we shared with our beloved pets.

It is important to approach these experiences

with an open heart and an open mind, allowing ourselves to feel the emotions that come with the loss of a furry family member.

By tuning into the signs and messages that our pets may be sending us, we may gain a deeper understanding of the ways in which they continue to be present in our lives.

For example, you may be sitting at home, lost in thought when suddenly you feel a sudden shift in air pressure. It may feel as though your pet is brushing past you, sending you a message of love and comfort from beyond.

While it may be difficult to process the emotions that come with the loss of a furry family member, moments like these can be incredibly powerful and can serve as a reminder of the unbreakable bond that exists between pets and their owners.

In these moments, it is important to take a deep breath, to allow yourself to feel the emotions that come with the loss of your pet, and to remember the love and joy that you shared together.

Signal 23

Seeing your pet's favorite place in your home can be a powerful sign of their presence in your life, even after they have passed on. It can bring back memories of the happy times you shared together, and can serve as a reminder that your pet's spirit is still with you in heaven.

Whether it's a cozy spot on the couch, a warm patch of sunlight on the floor, or a favorite bed, seeing your pet's favorite place can evoke a deep sense of nostalgia and longing. It can be a bittersweet experience, but also one that is filled with warmth and love.

For example, you may be cleaning your home when you come across your pet's favorite spot on the couch, complete with a little indent where they used to curl up and sleep.

Seeing this spot can be a poignant moment, bringing back memories of the countless times you sat together, watching TV or reading a book, and feeling the comfort of your pet's presence by your side.

These moments can be emotional and difficult to process, but they can also serve as a powerful reminder of the love and bond that you shared with your pet.

By embracing these signs and memories, you can find solace in the knowledge that your pet's spirit is still with you, watching over you from heaven.

In these moments, it's important to allow yourself to feel the emotions that come with the loss of your furry family member.

You may feel sadness, longing, or even joy as you remember the happy times you shared together.

By allowing yourself to feel these emotions, you can honor the memory of your pet and the special place they held in your heart.

Remember that while your pet may no longer be physically present in your home, their spirit lives on in the memories and moments that you shared together.

By embracing these signs of their presence, you can find comfort and peace in the knowledge that your beloved pet will always be with you in your heart.

Signal 24

Seeing your pet's face in a cloud can be a powerful and meaningful sign that their spirit is still with you, watching over you from heaven. It can be a truly breathtaking experience, and one that fills you with a sense of wonder and awe.

When you look up at the sky and see your pet's face in a cloud formation, it can feel like a miraculous and deeply personal moment.

You may feel a sense of comfort and peace, as if your pet is communicating with you and letting you know that they are still present in your life.

For example, you may be out for a walk on a sunny day when you look up and see a cloud that looks exactly like your beloved pet's face.

In that moment, you may feel a deep sense of connection and understanding, as if your pet is reaching out to you from beyond the veil to let you know that they are still with you in spirit.

These moments can be emotional and deeply moving, and they can serve as a powerful reminder of the love and bond that you shared with your pet.

By embracing these signs and moments, you can find solace in the knowledge that your pet's spirit is still with you, watching over you and bringing you comfort and peace.

In these moments, it's important to take a deep breath and allow yourself to fully experience the emotions that come with seeing your pet's face in a cloud. You may feel a deep sense of gratitude and joy, or you may feel a wave of sadness and longing.

Whatever emotions you feel, know that it's okay to embrace them and allow yourself to fully experience the moment.

Remember that your pet's spirit lives on in the world around you, and that they will always be with you in your heart.

By being open to these signs and embracing the emotions that come with them, you can find comfort and peace in the knowledge that your pet's love and presence will always be a part of your life.

Signal 25

Hearing the familiar sound of your pet's collar tag clinking can be a powerful reminder of the love and bond that you shared. It's a sound that is unique to your pet and one that can fill you with a sense of comfort and peace.

For example, you may be going about your day when you suddenly hear the distinct sound of your pet's collar tag clinking.

Even though your pet is no longer physically with you, the sound can bring them to mind and make you feel as if they are still by your side.

This can be a particularly powerful sign if you haven't heard the sound of your pet's collar tag in a while. It can feel like a gift from beyond the veil, a gentle reminder that your pet's spirit is still with you and that their love and presence will always be a part of your life.

In these moments, it's important to take a

deep breath and allow yourself to fully experience the emotions that come with hearing the sound of your pet's collar tag.

You may feel a sense of gratitude and joy, or you may feel a wave of sadness and longing.

Whatever emotions you feel, know that it's okay to embrace them and allow yourself to fully experience the moment.

Remember that your pet's love and presence will always be with you, even if they are no longer physically present.

By being open to these signs and embracing the emotions that come with them, you can find comfort and peace in the knowledge that your pet's spirit is still with you, watching over you and bringing you comfort and joy.

Signal 26

Seeing your pet's favorite blanket or bed can be a powerful sign that they are still with you, even though they have passed on. These items hold a special significance for your pet, and their presence can bring you comfort and peace.

For example, you may be going through your pet's belongings and come across their favorite blanket or bed. Seeing these items can fill you with a sense of nostalgia and a deep longing for your pet's physical presence.

However, it can also be a powerful reminder of the love and bond that you shared, and the happy memories that you created together.

In these moments, it's important to allow yourself to fully experience the emotions that come with seeing your pet's favorite blanket or bed.

You may feel a deep sense of loss and sadness,

or you may feel a sense of warmth and comfort from the memories that are brought to mind.

No matter what emotions you experience, know that your pet's spirit is with you, bringing you comfort and love.

By embracing these signs and allowing yourself to fully experience the emotions that come with them, you can find a sense of peace and comfort in the knowledge that your pet's love and presence will always be with you.

Remember that your pet's favorite blanket or bed is a special reminder of the bond that you shared, and the love that will always be a part of your life.

Embrace these signs and allow yourself to fully experience the emotions that come with them, and know that your pet's spirit is always with you, guiding and comforting you on your journey through life.

Signal 27

Hearing your pet's favorite sound or noise can be a powerful sign that they are still with you, even though they have passed on. These sounds may be unique to your pet and can bring back happy memories of the time you spent together.

For example, you may be sitting outside and hear a bird chirping in a certain way, which reminds you of the way your pet used to make a similar sound.

Or you may be doing household chores and suddenly hear a certain noise that your pet used to react to with excitement.

These moments can be bittersweet, as they remind you of the times you spent with your pet and how much they meant to you.

But they can also bring you comfort and joy, knowing that your pet's spirit is still with you and that they are continuing to share these moments with you from beyond the veil.

Allowing yourself to fully experience these signs and the emotions that come with them can be a healing experience.

You may feel a sense of nostalgia and longing, but you can also take comfort in the knowledge that your pet's love and presence continue to surround you.

Signal 28

When we lose our beloved pets, it can be hard to let go of their physical presence. However, even after they have crossed over, their energy remains and can often be felt by their human counterparts.

This energy can manifest in a variety of ways, from a warm sensation in the chest to a tingling feeling in the hands.

For some people, they may feel their pet's energy as a sudden surge of emotions or a sense of calm washing over them.

Others may experience physical sensations like a gentle nudge, a soft touch, or a warm breeze that seems to come out of nowhere. These signs can be comforting and remind us that our pets are still with us in a different form.

One example of feeling your pet's energy might be feeling a comforting presence in the room when you are feeling down or stressed.

You may feel as though someone is there with you, even though you know you are alone.

Another example could be feeling a gentle paw or nose nudge at a time when you need it most, almost as if your pet is trying to let you know they are still watching over you.

It's important to remember that these experiences are personal and unique to each individual.

Some may feel the presence of their pet frequently, while others may only feel it occasionally.

However, when these signs do occur, they can bring comfort and reassurance that our beloved pets are never truly gone, but always with us in spirit.

Signal 29

Seeing your pet's favorite color can be a powerful and meaningful sign of their continued presence and love in your life. Maybe your beloved furry friend had a favorite toy or collar that was a certain shade, or maybe you remember how their coat would catch the light in a certain way that made their fur look a particular color.

Whatever the connection, seeing that color after their passing can be a heartwarming reminder of the bond you shared.

For example, perhaps you're out for a walk and notice a flower in the exact shade of your pet's collar, or you come across a blanket in their favorite color that you never knew existed before.

These unexpected moments can be a comforting reminder that your pet is still with you in spirit, guiding you and reminding you of the love you shared.

And while it may seem like a small thing, the power of these signs can be immeasurable in helping to ease the pain of their absence and bring a sense of peace and comfort to your heart.

Signal 30

As we move through life after the loss of our beloved pets, we may experience sudden changes in energy around us, as if a wave of emotion is washing over us.

These changes in energy can come in the form of a sudden surge of happiness, a rush of peace and contentment, or even a fleeting moment of sadness.

These fluctuations may seem unexplainable at first, but they can often be attributed to the presence of our beloved pets in spirit.

It's not uncommon to feel a sudden shift in energy when our pets are near, as they bring with them an intense and unique energy that is unlike anything else in the world.

This energy can be felt in a number of ways, from a sudden warmth in your heart to a tingling sensation in your body.

It's important to trust these sensations and allow yourself to be open to the experience of your pet's energy around you.

Examples of feeling a sudden change in energy may include a sudden feeling of calm washing over you during a difficult time, or a sudden surge of happiness when thinking about a cherished memory with your pet.

It could also be a sudden burst of inspiration or motivation, as if your pet is encouraging you to pursue your dreams and goals.

Remember that the energy of our beloved pets is always with us, even after they have passed on from this world. By remaining open to the signs and signals that they are sending us, we can continue to feel their love and support in our lives.

Signal 31

The appearance of a butterfly or other symbol of transformation can be a powerful sign that your pet is still with you, even though they are no longer physically present.

The butterfly, in particular, is often seen as a symbol of transformation and rebirth, which can bring comfort and hope to those who are grieving the loss of their beloved pet.

When you see a butterfly or other symbol of transformation, take a moment to connect with the energy of your pet and feel their love and presence around you. Allow yourself to be open to the possibility that this is a sign from your pet, and that they are still with you in spirit.

Examples of seeing a butterfly or other symbol of transformation as a sign from a pet include finding a butterfly resting on your hand, seeing a caterpillar transform into a butterfly in your garden, or spotting a hummingbird or dragonfly that reminds you of your pet's spirit.

Remember that your pet's spirit is always with you, even though they may no longer be physically present.

By being open to the signs and messages they send, you can continue to feel their love and presence in your life, and find comfort in the knowledge that they are at peace in the afterlife.

Signal 32

When we lose our beloved pets, it can be difficult to find comfort in their absence. However, many people find that their pets continue to find ways to connect with them, even after they have passed on. One of these ways is by using nature as a means of communication.

Have you ever been on a walk and found yourself drawn to a particular tree or plant, only to realize that it was one of your pet's favorite spots?

Or maybe you notice that a certain flower or shrub that your pet used to love suddenly starts to bloom when you need it most. These can be powerful signs that your pet's spirit is still with you.

Some people even report feeling a sense of peace and comfort when they are near their pet's favorite nature spots. This can be a way for our pets to continue to provide us with comfort and guidance, even when they are no longer physically with us.

Examples of this include noticing that a certain tree in your backyard starts to bloom at the same time every year, which coincides with the anniversary of your pet's passing.

Or, perhaps you feel a sense of calm when you walk by a particular park bench that you used to sit on with your pet.

No matter how subtle or obvious these signs may be, they can bring great comfort to those who are grieving the loss of a pet.

It's important to stay open and receptive to these signs, as they can help us to feel connected to our pets and continue to carry their love and memory with us always.

Signal 33

Feeling a sense of peace or calm is a common sign that your pet is still with you in spirit. This can happen when you least expect it, but it's important to pay attention and embrace the moment.

It could be as simple as feeling a gentle breeze on your face, or as profound as suddenly feeling a sense of calm wash over you during a difficult time.

I remember feeling an overwhelming sense of peace when I was grieving the loss of my dog. It had been weeks since he passed, and I was still struggling to come to terms with it.

One day, as I was sitting outside in the garden, I suddenly felt a warm and comforting presence surround me.

I closed my eyes and took a deep breath, feeling a sense of peace wash over me. In that moment,

I knew that my dog was still with me and that everything was going to be okay.

Another example of feeling a sense of peace or calm can be when you visit a place that was special to you and your pet.

You may suddenly feel a sense of comfort and reassurance, as if your pet is telling you that they are still there with you, watching over you.

It's important to remember that everyone experiences grief differently, and the signs of our pets' presence can vary.

But if you do feel a sudden sense of peace or calm, embrace it and know that your pet is still with you, bringing comfort and love even from beyond the veil.

Signal 34

When we lose a beloved pet, it can be difficult to come to terms with their passing. However, many of us find comfort in the belief that our pets continue to exist in a spiritual form, waiting for us on the other side.

One of the most powerful symbols of crossing over is the image of the rainbow bridge, a bridge that connects the physical world with the world of the afterlife.

The rainbow bridge is said to be where pets go after they pass away, where they can play and wait for their owners to join them.

When we see a rainbow bridge or another symbol of crossing over, we may feel a sense of peace knowing that our pets are in a better place.

We may also feel a sense of hope, knowing that we will one day be reunited with our furry companions.

This can bring a great deal of comfort during the grieving process.

Examples of symbols of crossing over may include seeing a rainbow bridge in a painting, a tattoo, or a piece of jewelry.

It may also be a more subtle sign, such as the sight of a rainbow, which can symbolize a connection between the physical and spiritual worlds.

Additionally, some people may experience a sense of connection with their pets while visiting natural landscapes, such as a forest or a mountain, which can remind them of the beauty and wonder of the natural world.

Signal 35

When we lose a beloved pet, it can feel like a piece of our heart has been taken away. We may yearn for their comforting presence and long to hear their voice again.

While we may never hear their bark, meow, or chirp in the same way we once did, we may still hear echoes of their favorite word or phrase.

Maybe your dog would always perk up at the sound of "walk" or "treat," or your cat would come running at the mention of "kitty-kitty."

Even the sound of their name may still carry special meaning and comfort. Hearing these familiar words can be a sign that our pets are still with us in spirit, sending us messages of love and reassurance from beyond the veil.

One example of this is a woman who lost her beloved dog, who was always excited at the sound of the word "cookie."

After her dog passed away, she would hear the sound of a bell tinkling, like the one on her dog's collar, followed by the sound of her dog's name and the word "cookie."

This experience brought her immense comfort and reminded her that her dog was still with her in spirit.

Another example is a cat who was known to meow loudly when her name was called.

After her passing, her owner would occasionally hear a faint meowing sound coming from the direction of her cat's favorite resting spot, even though no other cats were present.

This subtle but powerful reminder helped her to feel connected to her beloved feline companion.

These experiences remind us that the love and connection we share with our pets can transcend physical form.

Even after they have crossed over, their spirit and energy continue to be present in our lives, offering us comfort, love, and guidance.

Signal 36

When we have a deep and loving bond with our pets, it can be hard to imagine life without them. Even after they've passed, the love and memories we shared with them continue to live on, and can often bring us a sense of comfort and peace during times of grief.

Sometimes, when we're feeling especially low, we may feel a sudden sense of warmth or love wash over us, as if our pet is right there with us, comforting us in their own special way.

It may be a sudden feeling of calm, or a memory that pops into our mind at just the right time, reminding us of the love and bond we shared with our beloved pet.

Other times, we may feel a sense of their energy or presence around us, almost as if they're still there, by our side, watching over us and providing us with the strength we need to carry on.

It's important to remember that the love and bond we share with our pets transcends time and space, and that they will always be with us in our hearts and memories.

Examples of feeling a sense of love or comfort from a pet's presence can include suddenly smelling their favorite scent or feeling a warm breeze brush against your skin.

It may also come in the form of a vivid dream or a sudden memory that makes you smile, even in the midst of your grief.

Signal 37

The sight of someone who reminds us of our beloved pet can bring about a flood of emotions and memories. Perhaps it's their favorite human, or maybe it's another pet they were particularly fond of.

Regardless, the presence of this individual can serve as a powerful reminder of our pet's impact on our lives.

For example, let's say your cat was particularly fond of your best friend, who would always come over and play with her. After your cat passed away, you might find comfort in spending time with your friend, reminiscing about your cat's funny quirks and playful antics.

Even if your friend isn't physically present, simply hearing their name or seeing a photo of them could evoke feelings of warmth and nostalgia.

Or maybe your dog loved to play with a neighbor's dog who would come over for frequent playdates.

After your dog's passing, seeing that other dog out on a walk or playing in the yard next door could be a bittersweet reminder of the fun times your dog had with their friend.

Whatever the case may be, these reminders of our pets' relationships can provide a sense of solace and connection. Even though our pets are no longer with us, the memories and love they shared with others continue to live on.

Seeing a white feather can be a comforting sign that our beloved pets are still with us in spirit. White feathers are often associated with purity, innocence, and protection, and they are thought to be a symbol of a guardian angel's presence.

When we come across a white feather unexpectedly, it can feel like a gentle reminder that our pets are watching over us from the other side.

For example, I remember one day when I was feeling particularly sad about the loss of my dog, I found a white feather on my doorstep.

It was as if my dog was telling me that everything was going to be okay and that he was still with me in spirit.

The appearance of white feathers can also be a sign of spiritual growth and transformation. They can remind us to let go of our grief and embrace the beauty of life, knowing that our pets are always with us in our hearts.

Signal 39

When we have a deep bond with our pets, it's not uncommon to feel a sense of joy or happiness when we think of them or sense their presence.

This can come in many different forms, such as a sudden burst of energy or a feeling of warmth in our hearts.

It's as though they are sending us a message that they are okay and that they want us to be happy.

One example of this is when I think of my cat, who passed away several years ago.

Even though it's been a while, I still feel a sense of joy when I remember her funny antics and loving personality.

I can almost hear her purring in my ear, and I know that she is still with me in spirit, bringing a smile to my face whenever I think of her.

Another example is when a friend of mine lost her dog, who was her constant companion for over a decade.

Despite the grief and pain of losing him, she often felt a sense of joy and comfort knowing that he was no longer suffering and that he was still with her in spirit.

She found that she could feel his presence in a comforting way, and that it brought her a sense of peace and happiness during a difficult time.

These moments of joy and happiness are reminders of the deep love and connection we share with our pets, and the profound impact they can have on our lives, even after they are gone.

Signal 40

Hearing your pet's voice in your mind can be a comforting and bittersweet experience. It's not uncommon for pet owners to hear their beloved pet's voice, even after they have passed on.

It may feel like a memory, a dream, or a visitation from beyond, but it can bring a sense of peace and comfort to know that your pet is still with you in some way.

Sometimes, it can be difficult to differentiate between your own thoughts and your pet's voice, but it's important to trust your instincts and embrace the experience.

You may hear your pet's voice saying their name, a favorite phrase, or even offering words of comfort during a difficult time.

For example, after her cat passed away, one pet owner often heard her cat's voice saying "I love you" during moments of stress or sadness. The sound of her cat's voice brought her comfort and reminded her of the love and bond they shared.

While hearing your pet's voice may feel like a small and fleeting experience, it can provide a sense of connection and reassurance that your pet's spirit and love lives on.

Signal 41

Seeing a shooting star or other symbol of wish fulfillment can be a powerful sign from your beloved pet. It can serve as a reminder that your pet's spirit is still with you, guiding you and looking out for you from beyond.

It can also be a symbol of hope and positivity, reminding you to keep a positive outlook and have faith that everything will work out for the best.

One example of this is when a pet owner saw a shooting star shortly after their pet passed away.

The owner was filled with grief and feeling lost without their pet, but seeing the shooting star brought a sense of comfort and reassurance that their pet was still with them in spirit.

It gave them hope and a renewed sense of faith that their pet was watching over them and guiding them.

Another example is when a pet owner saw a rainbow after a particularly difficult day of missing their pet. The rainbow reminded them of the beauty and love that their pet brought into their life, and gave them a sense of peace and comfort.

The owner felt that their pet's spirit was reaching out to them through the symbol of the rainbow, reminding them that they are never truly alone.

Overall, seeing a shooting star or other symbol of wish fulfillment can be a powerful reminder of the love and connection between you and your pet, even beyond their physical existence.

It can bring a sense of comfort, hope, and positivity during difficult times, and serve as a beacon of light to guide you through the darkness.

Signal 42

When we see the favorite animal of our beloved pet, it can be a powerful and emotional experience. We may feel a sudden surge of love and connection, as if our pet is sending us a message of comfort and reassurance.

For example, one day I was feeling particularly sad and missing my dog who had passed away. As I was walking outside, a squirrel suddenly appeared and started to follow me along the path.

He used to enjoy playing with squirrels by chasing them.

It seemed almost as if the squirrel was trying to communicate with me and lift my spirits. Seeing the squirrel brought me a sense of peace and comfort, as if my dog was saying, "I'm still here with you, and I love you."

Similarly, a friend of mine lost her cat and was struggling to come to terms with the loss.

One day, she was sitting in her backyard and noticed a butterfly fluttering around her. The butterfly was the same color that her cat enjoyed playing with, and she felt a sudden surge of love and connection.

It was as if her cat was sending her a message of love and reassurance, and it brought her a great deal of comfort and peace.

In these moments, it's important to trust our intuition and believe that our pets are still with us in spirit.

Even though they may no longer be physically present, their love and energy continue to surround us and guide us on our journey.

Signal 43

When we feel grateful, it means we are acknowledging the good things in our life and showing appreciation for them. When we feel this sense of gratitude towards our pets, it can be a powerful and uplifting experience.

It reminds us of the joy and love that our pets bring into our lives, and how lucky we are to have them.

There are many ways that we might feel a sense of gratitude towards our pets. Perhaps it's when they snuggle up to us on the couch after a long day, or when they greet us enthusiastically when we come home.

Maybe it's when they do something silly or unexpected that makes us laugh, or when they offer a paw or a nuzzle of comfort when we're feeling down.

Feeling gratitude towards our pets can also

come from reflecting on the memories and moments we've shared with them.

It might be the way they used to greet us at the door with their wagging tail or the sound of their purring as they snuggled into our lap.

Even in their absence, we can be grateful for the impact they've had on our lives and the memories we carry with us.

Gratitude can also be expressed in different ways, whether it's through a simple thank you or by doing something special for our pets, like taking them on a walk or giving them an extra treat.

By expressing our gratitude towards our pets, we deepen our connection with them and strengthen the bond we share.

In my own experience, I feel grateful for my pets every day.

Whether it's the way my cat curls up on my lap as I read or the way my dog greets me with a wagging tail when I come home, their presence brings me so much joy and comfort. I am grateful for their unconditional love and companionship, and I strive to show them my appreciation every day.

Signal 44

When we form a deep bond with our pets, we often learn their likes and dislikes, preferences and personalities.

It's common to give our pets compliments, to praise them for their loyalty, intelligence, and even physical attributes.

While our pets may not understand our words, they can pick up on our tone, body language, and energy.

Hearing our pet's favorite compliment can bring us comfort and help us remember the special moments we shared with them. It's a reminder of the love and joy they brought into our lives.

For example, I had a cat named Luna who was known for her beautiful, shiny coat. I would often compliment her on how sleek and elegant she looked.

After she passed away, whenever I saw another cat being complimented with the same praises I often used, I would be reminded of Luna and the special bond we shared.

Another example could be a dog who loves being called a good boy or girl. Hearing those words can make them feel appreciated and loved, and remind us of the happiness they brought into our lives.

In times of grief and loss, hearing our pet's favorite compliment can bring us a sense of comfort and connection to the special bond we shared.

It's a small but meaningful way to honor and remember our beloved pets.

Signal 45

As pet owners, we often seek comfort in the signs our beloved pets leave for us after they cross over the rainbow bridge. Seeing a heart or other symbol of love can be a powerful reminder that our pets are still with us in spirit and that their love transcends death.

When we see these symbols, we may feel a sense of warmth and reassurance that our pets are watching over us and sending their love from beyond.

It can bring us comfort in times of grief and help us feel connected to our pets even though they may no longer be physically present.

Examples of symbols of love can include hearts, butterflies, or even the shape of our pet's paw print. These symbols can appear in unexpected places, such as on a cloud or in the pattern of a leaf.

It is up to us to remain open to the signs and symbols our pets send us, and to cherish the love and memories we shared with them.

Signal 46

As pet owners, we know our pets have preferences, just like us. And when we see a view or scenery that our pets enjoyed, it can bring back happy memories and even a feeling of connection with them.

Perhaps it's a hiking trail or a scenic overlook that you and your pet used to visit frequently. Or maybe it's a window in your home that your cat always used to lounge in, enjoying the view outside.

When we see our pet's favorite view or scenery, it can be a comforting reminder that our pets are still with us in spirit. It's as if they are telling us, "I'm still here, enjoying this view with you." This can bring us a sense of peace and happiness, knowing that our beloved pets are still a part of our lives.

For me, seeing a specific tree in my backyard

always reminds me of my dog who loved to nap under it. When I see that tree, I can almost feel his presence and it's a bittersweet feeling that always brings a tear to my eye.

Examples:

- Every time I drive by the beach where I used to take my dog for walks, I can feel him by my side, enjoying the sea breeze and the sound of the waves crashing.
- Whenever I pass by the park where I used to take my cat to sunbathe, I can almost see her lounging in the grass, enjoying the warm sun on her fur.
- Seeing the mountains where I used to hike with my dog always brings a smile to my face as I remember the joy he had running around and exploring the trails.

Signal 47

Feeling a sense of humor or playfulness is a sign that your pet is still with you in spirit. It's their way of letting you know that they're happy and that they want you to be happy too. You might feel a sudden urge to laugh or smile for no apparent reason, or you might notice something funny that reminds you of your pet.

For example, you might be going through old photos of your pet and suddenly notice a funny expression or silly pose that you had forgotten about.

Or, you might be walking in the park and come across a dog doing something silly or playful that reminds you of your own pet.

Another example is if you hear a certain noise or sound that always made your pet playful or excited. It could be the sound of a toy, the jingle of a collar, or even a certain song or melody.

Hearing this can bring back happy memories and make you feel as though your pet is still with you.

It's important to embrace these moments of humor and playfulness, as they can help lift your spirits and remind you of the joy your pet brought into your life.

Cherish the memories and let yourself laugh and smile, knowing that your pet is still with you in spirit, always bringing happiness and love.

Signal 48

Seeing a dragonfly or other symbol of transformation can be a powerful experience that evokes a sense of change, growth, and renewal.

Dragonflies are often associated with transformation, change, and the cycles of life. When we see a dragonfly, it can be a reminder to embrace change and take a closer look at the areas in our lives where we may need to grow and evolve.

Similarly, other symbols of transformation, such as butterflies or caterpillars, can represent the transformation of our thoughts, emotions, or even our physical selves.

When we see these symbols, it can be a powerful reminder to trust in the process of growth and change, even when it feels uncomfortable or challenging.

In the context of our beloved pets, seeing a dragonfly or other symbol of transformation can be a reminder of their continuing presence in our lives, even after they have passed on.

It can be a powerful reminder that they are still with us, supporting us through our own journeys of growth and transformation.

For example, a person who recently lost their pet may be feeling stuck and unable to move forward. One day, they may see a dragonfly hovering near them and feel a sudden sense of peace and comfort.

Seeing the dragonfly may remind them of the love and support their pet gave them during their time together, and encourage them to embrace the changes and transformations they need to make in their own life.

Overall, seeing symbols of transformation can be a powerful reminder of the cyclical nature of life and the importance of embracing change and growth.

It can also be a comforting reminder of the continuing presence and support of our beloved pets, even after they have left this physical world.

Signal 49

Seeing your pet's favorite toy or object move on its own can be a powerful and emotional experience. It can be difficult to explain, but when you witness something like this, it can feel like your pet is still with you, even if they have already passed on.

I remember one such experience that I had with my cat, who had recently passed away. Her favorite toy was a little stuffed mouse that had a jingle bell inside.

One day, as I was sitting in my living room, I saw the mouse move across the floor on its own. At first, I thought it was just my imagination, but then I saw it move again. I felt a sense of joy and comfort wash over me, and I knew that my cat was still with me in some way.

Experiences like this are often dismissed as coincidence or imagination, but to those who have experienced them, they can be incredibly meaningful.

They offer a sense of connection and comfort that can be difficult to find in other ways.

Whether it's a favorite toy, a special place, or a certain sound, our pets often leave behind reminders of their presence in our lives.

And when we experience something that feels like a sign from them, it can be a powerful reminder of the love and bond that we shared.

Signal 50

As a pet lover, you may sometimes find yourself feeling a sudden surge of inspiration or creativity, and this could be a sign from your beloved pet.

When you are feeling stuck or in need of a creative boost, your pet may be guiding you with their energy and spirit.

For example, perhaps you are an artist who is struggling to come up with a new idea for a painting. You may suddenly feel your pet's presence around you, and a wave of inspiration washes over you.

Suddenly, you see an image in your mind's eye that you know would make a beautiful painting. This could be a sign that your pet is with you, supporting and encouraging your creativity.

Similarly, if you are a writer who is struggling to find the right words for a story, you may find that your pet's energy helps you to tap into your creativity and find the perfect words.

Or if you are a musician, you may find that your pet's energy helps you to write a new song or play a melody that you have never played before.

In these moments, it is important to trust your intuition and let your pet's energy guide you. Your pet may no longer be physically with you, but their spirit and energy continue to inspire you and help you to create beautiful things.

Signal 51

As pet owners, we all have our special moments and memories with our furry friends that we cherish. One of the most heartwarming experiences is hearing your pet's favorite activity or game, whether it be the sound of a squeaky toy or the rustling of leaves as they chase after a ball.

For me, hearing the sound of my dog's tail thumping against the floor in excitement as she anticipates our daily game of fetch always brings a smile to my face.

It's a sound that signifies pure joy and excitement, and it's a reminder of the special bond we share. It's not just dogs that have their favorite games, either.

Cats may enjoy the sound of a crinkling toy or the rustling of feathers as they play with their favorite wand.

Hearing these sounds can transport us to a

place of happiness and contentment, reminding us of the love and joy our pets bring into our lives.

These sounds can also bring us closer to our pets, helping us to understand their personalities and preferences.

By listening to their favorite activities, we can provide them with the best possible care and create even stronger bonds with them. In the end, the sound of our pets' favorite activity or game is a reminder of the love and joy they bring into our lives, and it's a special connection that we should cherish and celebrate.

Signal 52

As a pet lover, I know how much our furry friends bring joy and color to our lives.

There are moments when I'm out in nature and a burst of color catches my eye, reminding me of my pet's favorite color.

It's as if they're sending me a message of love and comfort.

Whether it's the bright blue of a clear sky or the rich green of the leaves on a tree, seeing these colors can bring a sense of peace and happiness.

It's as if our pets are telling us that they're with us, even if we can't see them physically.

One example of this was during a walk in the park when I saw a vibrant purple flower that reminded me of my cat's favorite toy.

It brought back memories of all the times we played together and made me feel grateful for the time we had.

Another time, I was feeling down and saw a bright yellow butterfly flutter by, reminding me of my dog's sunny personality.

Seeing that flash of yellow brought a smile to my face and made me feel like my dog was telling me to keep my chin up.

These moments of connection with our pets can come in unexpected ways, and it's up to us to be open to them.

When we take the time to appreciate the beauty around us, we can feel the love and presence of our pets even when they're not physically here.

Signal 53

As a pet owner, sometimes we may feel a sense of guilt or regret for things we may have done or not done for our beloved animal friends.

However, when we are in the presence of our pets, we often feel a sense of forgiveness and compassion, as they have an innate ability to bring out the best in us and to forgive us unconditionally.

Seeing our pets' faces and feeling their warm fur or soft feathers can instantly melt away any feelings of guilt or negativity. In their presence, we are reminded of their unconditional love, and our hearts open up to the possibility of forgiveness and redemption.

For example, I remember one time when I accidentally stepped on my dog's tail, causing him to yelp in pain. I felt so terrible and guilty, but as soon as he came over to me and wagged his tail, forgiving me, all of those negative emotions disappeared, and I was filled with a sense of love and gratitude.

Our pets teach us the importance of forgiveness and empathy, as they always seem to be able to look past our flaws and mistakes, and remind us that it's never too late to make things right.

Signal 54

As I was walking in the park the other day, I caught a glimpse of a majestic creature in the sky. It was a dragon, soaring effortlessly among the clouds. Although I knew it was not real, the sight filled me with a sense of wonder and awe.

Dragons have long been a symbol of power, and I couldn't help but think of my beloved pet and their own strength and resilience.

Just like a dragon, they have a fierce spirit and an unwavering determination that always inspires me.

Perhaps the dragon was a message from my pet, reminding me of their own power and encouraging me to tap into my own. Or perhaps it was just a reminder to keep dreaming and reaching for the impossible, just as my pet always did.

Either way, I felt grateful for the reminder and

for the love and strength that my pet brought into my life. Even in their absence, they continue to inspire me and bring magic and wonder to the world around me.

Signal 55

When I find myself in the bustling city, surrounded by tall buildings and the sound of traffic, I can't help but feel a twinge of sadness that my furry friend is no longer by my side to explore with me.

But every now and then, I catch a glimpse of something that reminds me of them, and I feel their presence once again.

Perhaps it's a park bench where we used to rest after a long walk, or a pet store window that they would always stop to gaze at. Or maybe it's a street performer playing their favorite song, or a busy café that they would have loved to people-watch from.

One time, I was walking down a busy street when I saw a dog that looked exactly like my beloved pet. Although it wasn't him, seeing that familiar face brought a smile to my face and reminded me of all the joy and love he brought to my life.

Even in the midst of the city's chaos, my pet's memory can bring me a sense of comfort and peace. It's as if he was saying to me, "I may not be here physically, but I'm still with you in spirit."

So when I see those little reminders of my pet in the city, I can't help but feel grateful for the time we had together and for the memories that will always stay with me.

Signal 56

As I go through life, there are moments when I feel like I am weighed down by the burdens of the world. But sometimes, there are fleeting moments of lightness, where I feel unencumbered, free, and liberated.

These moments can come unexpectedly, and sometimes they can be triggered by something as small as a sensation.

One such sensation is the feeling of freedom or liberation that comes over me when I see my pet running and playing in an open field.

There is something about the way they move with abandon, unrestrained by worries or fears, that fills me with a sense of joy and lightness.

It's not just in their movements either. The mere presence of my pet can also bring me a feeling of freedom. Their unconditional love and acceptance make me feel like I can be myself, without any pretense or hiding.

In their presence, I feel free to express my emotions, whether it be through laughter, tears, or anything in between.

These moments of freedom and liberation can also be found in other unexpected places. Maybe it's the feeling of the wind on my face as I ride my bike, or the rush of adrenaline as I try something new.

Whatever the source, these moments of freedom are precious reminders that there is always a path to feeling light and free, even in the midst of life's challenges.

Signal 57

As a pet owner, I believe that our pets have unique personalities and interests just like humans. Sometimes, we may find ourselves reminded of our beloved pets in unexpected ways, such as when we see their favorite book or movie.

When I catch a glimpse of my pet's favorite book or movie, I feel a sense of comfort and connection to them. It's almost as if they're right there with me, sharing in the experience.

Whether it's a children's book or an action-packed movie, seeing their favorite brings back happy memories of the times we spent together, cuddled up and enjoying each other's company.

For example, my dog absolutely adores the classic children's book, well, he loved chewing it, "Where the Wild Things Are" by Maurice Sendak.

Whenever I see a copy of the book in a store or in someone's home, I can't help but smile and think of my furry friend. It's a special connection that we share, and one that will always bring a little bit of joy into my day.

In those moments, I'm reminded of the unique bond I have with my pet and how much they bring to my life. Even though they may no longer be physically present, their memory lives on in the small moments that remind me of their favorite things.

Signal 58

When we hear the sound of our pets' laughter, it's like music to our ears. It's a sound that brings so much joy and happiness, and can instantly lift our spirits.

Our pets have a unique way of expressing themselves, and their laughter is just one of the ways they show their happiness and contentment.

The sound of my dog's laughter is something that will always stay with me. It's a high-pitched, almost wheezing sound that he makes when he's particularly happy or excited. It's a sound that I associate with good memories and happy times.

Sometimes, even after our pets have passed away, we can still hear their laughter in our minds. It's a reminder of the joy they brought to our lives and the happiness they experienced while they were with us.

It's a comforting thought that they are still

with us in some way, even if it's just through the memories and sounds they left behind.

When we hear our pets' laughter, it's important to cherish the moment and bask in the happiness it brings. It's a reminder of the bond we share with our furry friends and the love they have for us. It's a sound that can brighten even the darkest of days and bring a smile to our faces.

When we think of our beloved pets, it's natural to think of the ways in which they brought joy and beauty into our lives. And one way that our pets can continue to do so even after they've passed on is through the art that we have come to associate with them.

Seeing a piece of art that reminds us of our pets can be a powerful experience, and can bring back memories of the love and joy they brought into our lives.

Maybe it's a painting that perfectly captures the spirit of our pet, or a sculpture that reminds us of their playful nature. Perhaps it's a photograph that captures a moment that we shared together, or a piece of jewelry that we wear to keep them close to us.

Whatever it may be, seeing a piece of art that reminds us of our pets can bring us comfort and a sense of connection.

I remember seeing a painting of a golden retriever that reminded me so much of my childhood pet. The way the dog was depicted, with its wagging tail and happy expression, was so spot-on that it brought tears to my eyes.

It was as though my dog was alive again, and I could feel his presence with me in that moment.

Another time, I saw a sculpture of a cat that looked so much like my own feline companion. The way the artist had captured the cat's graceful movements and curious expression was so familiar to me, and I felt a sense of comfort knowing that my pet was still with me in some way.

Whether it's a painting, sculpture, photograph, or any other form of art, seeing something that reminds us of our pets can bring us a sense of peace and comfort.

It's a reminder that even though they may no longer be with us physically, the love and memories we have of them will always be a part of our lives.

Signal 60

When I feel a sense of guidance or direction, it's like the universe is whispering to me, leading me in the right direction. It's a feeling that I can't ignore, and it brings me a sense of peace and calmness. It's almost like having a trusted friend by my side, helping me navigate life's ups and downs.

Sometimes, when I'm feeling lost or unsure about the path I'm on, I'll catch a glimpse of my pet out of the corner of my eye. It's as if they're telling me that everything will be okay and that I'm on the right track.

Other times, I'll feel a sudden gust of wind or see a butterfly fly past me, and I just know that I need to follow my heart and trust in the journey.

One example of this happened to me when I was deciding whether or not to take a new job opportunity. I was feeling hesitant and unsure about the decision, but one day, as I was walking through the park with my dog, I saw a flock of birds flying in a V-formation.

It was a beautiful sight, and I felt a sudden sense of clarity wash over me. I knew in that moment that I needed to take the chance and go for the job, and it ended up being one of the best decisions I've ever made.

So, when you feel that sense of guidance or direction, pay attention to the signs around you. Your pet, nature, and the universe may be trying to lead you on a path towards happiness and fulfillment.

Trust in yourself, trust in the journey, and trust in the signs that come your way.

Signal 61

As I gaze upon the delicate fluttering of a hummingbird, my heart is filled with a sense of joy and wonder. These tiny, colorful creatures are a symbol of happiness and lightness, and their presence can be a reminder of the beauty and magic that surrounds us.

For pet owners, seeing a hummingbird may hold an even deeper significance. It can be a sign that our beloved pets are still with us, and that their spirits continue to bring joy and positivity into our lives.

When I see a hummingbird, I am reminded of my dear furry friend who brought so much happiness and laughter into my life. It's as if they are saying, "I'm still here with you, and I always will be." It brings me comfort and a sense of peace to think of them in this way.

The appearance of a hummingbird can also be

a reminder to live in the moment and appreciate the simple things in life.

Just like the fleeting flutter of their wings, our time with our pets is precious and should be cherished.

In this way, a hummingbird can be a powerful symbol of both joy and loss, and a source of inspiration to live our lives to the fullest, with the love and memories of our furry companions always in our hearts.

Signal 62

Looking up at the night sky and seeing a constellation that reminds me of my pet can be a beautiful and emotional experience.

The stars and their arrangement can bring back happy memories and fill me with a sense of comfort, knowing that my beloved pet is still with me in some way.

The twinkling lights seem to form shapes that can represent my pet's features, making me feel as though they are looking down on me from the heavens above.

One constellation that reminds me of my pet is Canis Major, the constellation that contains the bright star Sirius, also known as the "Dog Star".

The shape of this constellation, resembling a dog, always brings a smile to my face and makes me feel as though my pet is nearby, watching over me.

It's a reminder of the joy and love that they brought into my life, and the connection that we shared.

Another constellation that reminds me of my pet is Leo, the lion. While not directly related to pets, the image of the lion is a symbol of strength and courage, qualities that my pet embodied.

Seeing this constellation can bring me a sense of inspiration, reminding me to embody those same qualities in my own life.

Regardless of the constellation, the feeling of seeing a pattern of stars that reminds me of my pet is a comforting and special experience.

It's a reminder of the bond that we shared and the love that still lives on, even in the stars.

Signal 63

As I go about my day, there are times when I feel a sense of intuition or insight that is difficult to explain.

It's as if a sudden burst of understanding fills my mind and guides me towards a certain direction.

This feeling can be subtle, like a gentle nudge in a certain direction, or it can be overpowering, like a wave that sweeps me off my feet.

When I feel this sense of intuition, I often think of my pet and how they seemed to have an uncanny ability to understand my moods and needs.

It's as if they could read my mind and were always there for me, offering support and guidance without ever uttering a word.

Perhaps it's this connection I shared with my

pet that has heightened my own sense of intuition.

When I feel lost or uncertain, I can't help but think of my pet and how they always seemed to know exactly what to do. It's as if their presence still lingers, guiding me on my journey.

Examples of feeling a sense of intuition or insight might include having a sudden realization about a problem you've been struggling with, or feeling a strong urge to pursue a new opportunity or direction in life.

It might also manifest as a feeling of comfort or calm in the midst of a difficult situation, as if your pet's spirit is there with you, providing guidance and support.

Signal 64

As a pet owner, there are certain sounds that instantly catch our attention and bring a smile to our face. One of these sounds is the familiar bark or meow of our beloved furry friends. But what happens when we hear a similar bark or meow pattern, one that reminds us of our own pet, yet we know it's not them?

For me, this often happens when I'm out for a walk and I hear a dog bark in a certain way that is reminiscent of my own dog's bark.

Even though I know it's not my dog, I can't help but turn my head and listen for a few seconds longer. It's almost as if my brain is trying to decipher the message that this other dog is communicating.

These moments remind me of the special bond that we share with our pets. The unique patterns and sounds of their barks, meows, or chirps are like a language that only we can understand.

And even when we hear these sounds in other animals, our intuition and love for our own pets make us pay attention and listen closely.

It's also a reminder of the community we share with other pet owners. We all have our own special companions, but we also share a love and appreciation for all animals.

When I hear a similar bark or meow pattern from a different animal, it's like a nod from the universe that we are all connected in some way.

In those moments, I feel a sense of gratitude and joy for the special bond I share with my pet, as well as the wider community of pet owners and animal lovers.

It's a beautiful reminder of the power of connection and the love that animals bring into our lives.

Signal 65

Seeing similar spots and discolorations can evoke a range of emotions for pet owners. It can be a reminder of our pet's unique physical characteristics or a reminder of their health struggles.

I've experienced this firsthand with my own pets.

One of my cats has a distinctive white spot on his back that sets him apart from his siblings. Whenever I see another cat with a similar spot, it reminds me of my own beloved feline and brings a smile to my face. It's almost as if I'm seeing a little piece of him in that other cat.

On the other hand, seeing similar discolorations or marks can also be a reminder of health issues. My dog has a distinct black spot on his tongue that is relatively uncommon.

When I see another dog with a similar mark, it

can make me think about my own dog's health and well-being. It can be a bittersweet reminder of the unique challenges we face as pet owners.

Overall, seeing similar spots and discolorations on other animals can be a powerful reminder of the special bond we share with our own pets. It can evoke a range of emotions, from joy to sadness, but ultimately serves as a testament to the deep love and connection we have with our furry companions.

Signal 66

As a pet owner, seeing a familiar breed of my pet on a TV show or movie can bring about a unique sense of connection and excitement.

It's as if the universe is speaking directly to me, and I'm meant to pay attention. I may find myself feeling more present and engaged with the show or movie, simply because I see my beloved pet reflected back at me.

When I see a pet that looks like mine on a screen, it can also spark memories of happy moments spent with my own furry friend. I may recall the feeling of their soft fur under my fingers or the sound of their joyful bark.

Even if the pet on the screen is just an actor, their presence can be enough to transport me back to moments of love and connection with my own pet.

Additionally, seeing a similar breed on TV or

in a movie can offer a sense of validation or pride in my own pet. It's a reminder that my pet is a part of a larger community, with their own unique personality and characteristics.

It can make me feel like I'm part of something bigger, and that there are others out there who understand the special bond I share with my pet.

For example, if I have a Golden Retriever and I see one on a movie, I might feel more connected to the character and the story, or feel proud and grateful to have a dog like my own.

It could also remind me of moments spent playing fetch or snuggling with my own furry friend, bringing me a sense of warmth and joy.

In this way, seeing a similar breed on a screen can be a small but meaningful moment of connection and joy for a pet owner.

Signal 67

As I sit here, I close my eyes and take a deep breath, feeling the calmness slowly washing over me. It's as if all the chaos of the world has dissipated, and I'm left with a sense of pure tranquility.

This feeling of serenity is something that I often experience when I am near my pet.

There is something about being in the presence of my furry friend that makes me feel centered and grounded. Whether I'm cuddling with them on the couch or simply watching them play, their presence seems to slow down time and help me connect to a deeper sense of peace.

It's almost as if my pet has a magical power to calm my restless mind and soothe my anxious heart. Their gentle purrs, soothing presence, and unconditional love all contribute to this profound sense of serenity that I feel in their company.

The feeling of serenity that my pet brings to my life is something that I am incredibly grateful for. In moments of stress and chaos, I can always turn to them for comfort and find solace in their calming presence. It's as if they hold the key to a peaceful, centered way of being that I strive to embody in my daily life.

In a world where we are constantly bombarded with noise and distractions, having a sense of serenity is truly a gift. And for me, that gift is embodied in the loving, peaceful presence of my pet.

Signal 68

As a pet owner, I know that sometimes even the slightest mention of your pet's favorite place or location can trigger a wave of emotions.

The sound of someone else mentioning that special spot can instantly transport you to memories of joyful times spent with your furry friend.

Perhaps it's the mention of a local park where you and your dog used to take long walks, or the name of the beach where your cat would lay in the sun.

Hearing those words can bring back vivid memories of their wagging tail or soft purring, the warmth of the sun on their fur, and the feeling of contentment you shared together.

Even if it's just a passing comment from a stranger or a reference in a book or movie, hearing the name of that special place can make your heart swell with love for your pet and gratitude for the memories you shared.

It's a powerful reminder that our pets continue to impact our lives, even after they're gone.

For example, when I heard a colleague mention a local dog park in a conversation, memories of my late dog came flooding back.

I could almost feel his presence, running ahead of me with his tail wagging and his tongue lolling out, as if he was still by my side.

It brought tears to my eyes but also a sense of comfort knowing that he had left such an impact on my life.

That's the beauty of our pets' legacies - they remain with us long after they've crossed the rainbow bridge.

Signal 69

As a pet owner, I know how important it is to make our furry companions feel loved and comfortable.

One of the ways we do that is by providing them with their favorite things, including clothing.

Seeing our pets in their favorite piece of clothing can bring us a sense of joy and happiness, knowing that we've provided them with something they truly enjoy.

For example, my cat has a favorite sweater that she loves to wear during the colder months. Whenever I see her snuggled up in it, it warms my heart to know that she's comfortable and happy. It also brings back memories of when I first got the sweater for her and how excited she was to wear it.

The sight of our pets in their favorite clothing can also be a source of entertainment and amusement.

Whether it's a dog in a silly hat or a cat in a fancy dress, seeing them dressed up can bring a smile to our faces and make us laugh.

In some cases, seeing our pets in their favorite clothing can also help us understand their personalities better.

For example, if your dog always chooses to wear a bandana with a particular pattern or color, it may indicate their preference for certain colors or patterns.

Overall, seeing our pets in their favorite clothing is a simple pleasure that can bring us closer to them and deepen our bond.

It's a reminder that the little things we do for them can make a big difference in their happiness and well-being.

Signal 70

Sometimes I feel a sudden sense of connection or unity, as if I am deeply in tune with the world around me. It's a feeling that fills me with joy and wonder, as if I am a part of something much bigger and more profound than myself.

This feeling can come from many different sources, but often it is triggered by the presence of my pets.

When I'm snuggled up on the couch with my furry friends, I can feel their warmth and their energy, and I know that we are connected on a deep level.

We share a bond that goes beyond words and touches the very essence of our beings. This connection can be felt not just with my pets, but with all animals and even with nature itself.

I often experience this sense of connection and unity when I am out in nature, surrounded by trees, flowers, and wildlife. I can feel the rhythm of the natural world and sense the energy that flows through it. It's as if everything is connected, and I am just a small part of a larger, more beautiful whole.

This feeling of unity can also come from moments of kindness and compassion.

When I see someone helping another person or an animal in need, it reminds me that we are all in this together, that we all have the capacity to love and care for one another.

In these moments of connection and unity, I am reminded of the power of love and the beauty of life. I am grateful for the chance to be a part of it all and to share in this experience with my pets and with all living beings.

Signal 71

When we lose a beloved pet, we can feel as if we've lost a part of ourselves. We long for a sign, a message, anything to let us know that our pets are still with us in some way. And sometimes, we are lucky enough to receive just that.

One such sign could come in the form of a paw print or nose print left behind by our pets. It could be on a piece of paper, on a piece of clothing, or even on a surface in our home.

Seeing that unmistakable imprint can be a powerful and emotional experience, bringing a sense of comfort and reassurance that our pets are still present in some way.

When I lost my dog, I was heartbroken and missed him terribly. One day, while going through his things, I found a t-shirt with his paw print on it.

It brought back so many memories of him and

reminded me of how much he meant to me.

Whenever I wear the shirt, I feel like he is still with me, and it brings me a sense of peace and comfort.

These signs may seem small, but they can hold immense meaning for us.

They remind us that our pets will always be a part of us and that their love will continue to guide us, even in their physical absence.

So the next time you come across a paw print or nose print from your pet, take a moment to cherish it and hold onto the connection it brings.

It's a reminder that the bond you share with your pet transcends physical boundaries and will last forever.

Signal 72

Feeling soft nibbles on my skin is a familiar sensation that reminds me of my beloved pet. The gentle pressure of their teeth on my hand or arm can bring back happy memories of playing and cuddling with them. It's a comforting feeling, like a small but significant piece of them is still with me.

When I feel those gentle nibbles, it's as if my pet is reaching out to me in their own unique way. Maybe they sense that I'm missing them, or perhaps they just want to say hello. Whatever the reason, those little bites make me feel like my pet is still by my side, even when they're physically gone.

Sometimes, those nibbles can be felt in unexpected ways. For example, I might feel a soft pinch on my arm when I'm sitting on the couch, or a slight pressure on my foot as I'm walking through the house. It's a fleeting sensation, but one that fills me with warmth and happiness.

These nibbles are a reminder of the bond between me and my pet, and the love and affection we shared. Even though they're no longer physically here, their memory lives on, and these small gestures help keep their spirit alive in my heart.

Signal 73

Feeling a sense of security or protection can come from many different sources in life. Sometimes, it can come from a physical presence, like the reassuring touch of a loved one or the solid strength of a reliable companion.

Other times, it can come from an inner sense of knowing that everything is going to be alright, even in the midst of uncertainty.

For many people, pets can provide an invaluable sense of security and protection.

Whether it's a loyal dog who is always by your side, a cuddly cat who nuzzles up against you when you're feeling down, or any other animal who provides a calming presence, our pets can make us feel safe and protected in a way that nothing else can.

I've experienced this feeling of security and protection many times in my life with my own pets. For example, I remember a time when I was feeling particularly vulnerable and anxious after a difficult day at work.

As soon as I walked through the door, my dog ran up to me, tail wagging, and nuzzled his head into my hand. In that moment, I felt a wave of relief wash over me - I knew that no matter what else happened, I had a loyal companion by my side who would always be there for me.

Similarly, I know many people who find comfort and security in the presence of their cats. There's something about the quiet, steady purr of a contented cat that can help to calm our nerves and ease our worries. Just knowing that our feline friends are nearby can help us to feel protected and secure, even when the world around us feels uncertain.

Ultimately, feeling a sense of security and protection is essential for our well-being.

With our pets by our side, we can face the world with a greater sense of calm and confidence, knowing that we have a loyal companion who will always be there to provide support and comfort.

Signal 74

When we catch a glimpse of a phoenix or any other symbol of rebirth, it can be a powerful reminder that new beginnings are possible, and that we have the strength to rise from the ashes of our past experiences.

The image of a phoenix rising from the ashes has been a potent symbol of renewal for centuries, inspiring people to see the possibility of growth and transformation even in the darkest of times.

For many pet owners, the sight of a phoenix can be a poignant reminder of the loss of a beloved pet, and a symbol of the hope that one day, they may find themselves in a place of healing and renewal.

It may also serve as a reminder that our pets, too, have the ability to bring light and hope into our lives, even when we are struggling.

For me, seeing a phoenix reminds me of a

time when I was going through a difficult period in my life, after the loss of my pet. One day, while walking in the park, I saw a beautiful phoenix mural painted on the wall.

It caught my eye and filled me with a sense of awe and inspiration. I felt a sense of hope and reassurance that, like the phoenix, I could rise again, that I could heal and move forward.

Symbols like the phoenix can act as powerful guides, helping us to tap into our inner strength and resilience.

They can serve as reminders that we are capable of transformation and growth, no matter what we may be facing.

So the next time you see a phoenix or other symbol of rebirth, take a moment to connect with its message, and allow it to inspire you to rise from the ashes and embrace the new beginnings that are waiting for you.

Signal 75

When we see our pets experience joy and contentment, it can bring a sense of warmth and happiness to our hearts.

Whether it's watching them play in the sun, run through the rain, or feel the gentle breeze on their fur, seeing our pets interact with nature is a reminder of the simple joys in life.

One particular aspect of nature that may catch our pet's attention is the weather.

Some pets enjoy the warmth of the sun and will bask in its rays for hours on end, while others may prefer the coolness of a crisp autumn day.

Our pets' love for different types of weather can be a source of inspiration and enjoyment for us.

When I see my pet enjoying their favorite type of weather, I am reminded of how much joy they can find in the little things in life.

It's a reminder to me to slow down and appreciate the beauty around us, no matter how small or seemingly insignificant.

For example, my dog absolutely loves the snow. Whenever he sees it falling from the sky, he immediately wants to run outside and play in it.

Watching him frolic in the snow, tail wagging and tongue lolling out of his mouth, fills me with a sense of joy and contentment.

Seeing him enjoy the winter weather in his own way is a reminder to me to find joy in the present moment and to appreciate the small moments of happiness that life brings.

Signal 76

As humans, we often find ourselves facing situations that challenge our beliefs, values, and perspectives. Sometimes, it can be difficult to accept and tolerate those who hold different opinions or ways of living.

However, when we cultivate a sense of acceptance and tolerance, we are able to embrace diversity and find common ground with others.

When I feel a sense of acceptance and tolerance, I feel a sense of inner peace and harmony. I feel more connected to those around me, and I am able to empathize and understand their perspectives.

This sense of acceptance allows me to see beyond differences and recognize the shared humanity that we all possess.

For pet owners, this sense of acceptance and tolerance can also extend to our furry companions.

Just like humans, pets have their own unique personalities, quirks, and preferences. When we accept and tolerate these differences, we are better able to build strong, meaningful relationships with our pets.

For example, if your pet has a fear or aversion to certain types of noises or environments, accepting and accommodating their needs can help them feel more comfortable and secure.

If your pet has certain behavioral issues, being patient and understanding can help you work through those challenges together.

Ultimately, a sense of acceptance and tolerance is about embracing the differences that make us unique, and recognizing that those differences are what make life interesting and beautiful.

When we learn to accept and tolerate others, including our pets, we create a more compassionate and inclusive world.

Signal 77

As I catch a glimpse of my pet's name on something, whether it be a collar or a food bowl, a deep sense of connection and joy arises within me. It's as if my beloved companion is right beside me, even when they are not physically present.

Seeing my pet's name on everyday objects serves as a reminder of the unique bond we share. It brings back cherished memories of all the times we spent together, playing, cuddling, and exploring.

Each time I see their name, I'm flooded with a sense of warmth and comfort, knowing that they are a significant part of my life and always will be.

It's these little moments of recognition that truly make me appreciate the bond I share with my pet. And it's not just me - many pet owners feel the same way.

Seeing our pets' names on things helps to

strengthen our emotional connection with them, even when they are not around. It's a powerful feeling, knowing that our pets are always with us in spirit, even when we can't physically be together.

For me, seeing my pet's name on things is a constant reminder of the love and joy they bring into my life. It's a small, but meaningful reminder that helps to deepen my bond with my furry companion.

Signal 78

When we form a bond with our pets, we often become curious about their unique personalities and traits. One way to gain insight into our pets is through their zodiac sign, a symbolic representation of their character based on their birth date.

Seeing your pet's zodiac sign mentioned and read can be a powerful experience, as it can provide a deeper understanding of their behavior and temperament.

For example, a pet born under the sign of Leo may be outgoing, affectionate, and playful, while a pet born under the sign of Virgo may be more reserved, detail-oriented, and independent.

Knowing your pet's zodiac sign can also help you better connect with them and tailor your interactions to their individual needs.

In my own experience, I have a cat born under

the sign of Taurus, and I have found her to be very stubborn and set in her ways, yet also deeply affectionate and loyal.

I've noticed that she tends to be more receptive to physical touch and loves being stroked and cuddled, which aligns with Taurus' association with sensuality and pleasure.

Seeing my pet's zodiac sign mentioned and read has also given me a deeper appreciation for the unique qualities that make her who she is.

While every pet is different and can't be defined solely by their zodiac sign, understanding this aspect of their personality can add another layer of richness to our relationships with them.

Overall, seeing your pet's zodiac sign mentioned and read can be a powerful sign that they are communicating with you. They're saying that they're always with you.

Signal 79

Sometimes I am struck with a sense of wonder and awe that fills me with amazement and admiration. It is as if the world suddenly reveals itself to me in a new light, and I am overwhelmed by its beauty and complexity.

In these moments, I feel a sense of humility and reverence, as if I am but a small part of something much greater than myself.

One of the most profound experiences that can evoke a sense of wonder is being in the presence of nature.

Whether it's watching a majestic sunset, walking through a lush forest, or staring up at a starry sky, the beauty and magnificence of the natural world can leave us feeling small and insignificant in the most wonderful way.

Our pets can also evoke this feeling, as we marvel at their unique personalities, quirks, and abilities that we never knew existed.

Another source of wonder can be found in the accomplishments of others. When we witness someone else's hard work, determination, and success, we are filled with a sense of awe and inspiration.

This can range from watching a child take their first steps to seeing someone achieve a long-sought-after dream, and it reminds us of the incredible power of the human spirit.

In all of these experiences, we are reminded of the vastness and complexity of the world around us, and how much there is still to discover and learn.

We are humbled by the greatness of it all, and at the same time, inspired to continue exploring and pushing our own boundaries.

So next time you find yourself in a moment of wonder and awe, take a deep breath and allow yourself to be fully present in that moment.

Let the feeling wash over you and fill you with a sense of appreciation and reverence for the world and all that it contains.

Signal 80

Seeing a pet with the same name as yours can be a powerful sign that your beloved companion is communicating with you from beyond. It can evoke a range of emotions, from comfort to confusion, and can leave you feeling both validated and curious.

When we lose a pet, it's not uncommon to wonder if their spirit is still with us. Signs and messages can come in many forms, including seeing another animal with the same name as your pet. While it may seem like a coincidence at first, it can be a deeply meaningful sign that your pet is still present in some way.

This sign can be particularly powerful if the name is unusual or specific to your pet. For example, if you had a pet named "Baxter" and you see another dog with the same name, it can be a powerful reminder of your bond with your pet and a validation that their spirit is still with you.

It's important to trust your intuition when it comes to signs like these. While some may dismiss them as mere coincidences, the power of these messages lies in their ability to provide comfort and healing during difficult times.

Remember that the love and connection you shared with your pet transcends physical boundaries, and signs like these can serve as a reminder that their spirit is always with you.

Signal 81

Seeing a sign or message with your pet's favorite toy or object in it can be a powerful and emotional experience. It may feel like a direct message from your beloved pet, reminding you of their presence and their special place in your heart.

Perhaps you're walking in the park and you suddenly see a flyer for a lost pet with a photo of a similar toy your pet loved. Or maybe you receive a social media post or message from a friend who spotted a similar toy at a pet store.

These signs can feel like your pet is communicating with you, letting you know that they are still with you in spirit and watching over you.

In these moments, it's natural to feel a rush of emotions, including joy, sadness, and longing. You may find yourself reminiscing about the memories you shared with your pet and feeling grateful for the time you had together.

It's important to honor these feelings and allow yourself to grieve in your own way.

At the same time, seeing these signs can also provide a sense of comfort and peace. It can be a reminder that your pet is always with you, even if they are no longer physically by your side.

It can also be a reminder to cherish the memories you have with your pet and to keep their spirit alive in your heart.

Ultimately, the experience of seeing a sign or message with your pet's favorite toy or object is unique to each individual and pet. It's a deeply personal and emotional experience that can bring a sense of connection and comfort during times of grief and longing.

Signal 82

Seeing a pack of dogs or a clowder of cats with the same breed as your deceased pet can be a powerful experience. It can stir up emotions of nostalgia, longing, and even hope.

The sight of these animals can remind you of the special bond you shared with your pet and bring back cherished memories. It can also be a sign that your pet's spirit is still present and watching over you.

When I saw a pack of dogs with the same breed as my beloved dog who had passed away, I felt a sudden jolt of emotion. It was as if my heart skipped a beat and then filled with love and longing.

The sight of those dogs reminded me of the special bond I shared with my pet and how much I missed him. But at the same time, it also gave me a sense of comfort and hope that he was still with me in some way.

Similarly, when my friend saw a clowder of cats with the same breed as her beloved cat who had passed away, she was moved to tears.

The sight of those cats brought back memories of her pet and the joy he brought into her life. It was as if her cat was sending a message of comfort and love from beyond the veil.

In these moments, it is important to allow yourself to feel the emotions that come up and to honor the memory of your pet.

Seeing a pack of dogs or a clowder of cats with the same breed as your deceased pet can be a powerful reminder that the bond you shared with your pet is eternal and that they are always with you in spirit.

Signal 83

When we lose a beloved pet, it can feel like a part of us is missing. We long for any sign that our pet is still with us in spirit, and sometimes those signs come in unexpected forms.

One such sign can be seeing a random animal feel at ease with us, as if they were sent by our departed pet to comfort us.

This experience can feel both surreal and comforting. It's as if the animal recognizes us, knows our grief, and offers us a small glimpse of the love and joy that our pet brought to our lives.

The animal may come close to us, nuzzle us, or even allow us to pet them, as if our pet's spirit is guiding them to offer us the affection that we miss so much.

For me, this sign came in the form of a stray cat. I was sitting outside on a bench, thinking about my recently departed dog, when a small black and white cat jumped up onto the bench next to me.

I was surprised, but the cat seemed completely comfortable with my presence. It curled up next to me and purred contentedly as I petted it. I felt a sudden warmth in my heart, as if my dog's spirit had sent this cat to comfort me in my time of need.

Of course, there could be many explanations for a random animal being at ease with us, but in those moments when we're missing our pets the most, it can be a profound and meaningful experience to believe that our pets are reaching out to us in this way.

It reminds us that even though they're no longer with us physically, the love and connection we shared with them lives on in spirit, and that they will always be a part of us.

Signal 83

When we lose a beloved pet, it can be a challenging and emotional experience. We often long for a way to feel connected to them, to know that they are still with us in some way.

And while we may not be able to see or touch them anymore, there are signs that they may be communicating with us from beyond.

One such sign is when we notice a random animal staring at us with intent. This may be a bird perched on a windowsill or a squirrel sitting on a nearby branch, watching us closely.

While we may initially dismiss this as coincidence or the animal's natural curiosity, it can actually be a sign that our pet is trying to reach out to us.

In my own experience, after the passing of my cat, I noticed a stray cat who would sit outside my window and stare at me for long periods of time.

At first, I didn't think much of it, but as time went on, it became a regular occurrence. I began to feel a sense of comfort and connection when I saw the stray, as if it was a sign that my cat was still with me in some way.

Seeing a random animal staring at you can be a powerful reminder that your pet's spirit is still present in the world. It may bring a sense of peace and comfort, or it may simply be a comforting reminder that they are never truly gone.

Whether it's a bird, squirrel, or stray cat, try to embrace the moment and allow yourself to feel a sense of connection to your beloved pet.

Signal 84

Sometimes, the universe sends us unexpected signs that our pet is still with us in spirit.

One such sign could be a person you barely know assuming that you have a pet.

This can happen in a variety of ways, such as a stranger striking up a conversation with you about their own pet, or a new acquaintance asking about your furry friend before you even have a chance to mention them.

These encounters may seem like mere coincidences, but they can hold a deeper meaning.

It's as if our pets are communicating to these strangers, letting them know that we are a pet owner and in need of comfort or support.

Perhaps they are guiding these individuals to us, helping us to connect with like-minded individuals who can empathize with our loss.

I experienced this myself shortly after the passing of my cat. I went to a coffee shop and struck up a conversation with the barista, who shared with me her own experience of losing a pet.

She was kind, understanding, and offered me a sense of comfort that I desperately needed in that moment. It felt as though my cat had led me to her, so that I could receive the support I needed.

These signs can be small, but they can provide a sense of connection and hope during a difficult time.

We may never know why or how our pets are able to communicate with the world around us, but we can take comfort in the fact that they are still with us in some way, and that their love and presence continue to surround us.

Signal 85

One possible sign that our deceased pet is communicating with us is the unexpected opportunity to adopt a new pet.

It may seem coincidental, but I believe that our pets have a way of guiding us to the animals that need us the most. Maybe we weren't even considering adopting a pet at the time, but then a friend or family member tells us about a cat or dog that needs a home.

Or we stumble upon a shelter while running errands and feel drawn to a certain animal. These opportunities may come out of nowhere and catch us off guard, but they can also bring a sense of comfort and purpose.

Adopting a new pet can never replace the one we lost, but it can provide a new source of joy and love in our lives. Our deceased pet may be trying to tell us that it's okay to open our hearts again, and that they want us to experience the joy of a new pet.

I experienced this firsthand when my beloved dog passed away. I was heartbroken and didn't think I could ever open my heart again to another pet.

However, a few weeks later, a friend asked me to help find a home for a stray dog that had wandered into their yard. As soon as I saw the dog, I felt a connection with him that I couldn't explain.

It was like my deceased dog had sent him to me as a sign. I ended up adopting the stray dog, and although he was very different from my previous pet, he brought a whole new kind of joy and love into my life.

In summary, the unexpected opportunity to adopt a pet can be a powerful sign that our deceased pet is communicating with us.

While it may be difficult to open our hearts to a new pet at first, it can bring a sense of purpose and joy that our deceased pet may want us to experience.

Signal 86

One way they may communicate with you is through the actions of other animals, such as our neighbor's pets. If you have recently experienced the loss of a pet and find that a neighbor's pet suddenly seems more affectionate towards you, this could be a sign that your pet is communicating with you.

Perhaps your neighbor's cat, who normally keeps to herself, suddenly comes to your doorstep and nuzzles your hand. Maybe your neighbor's dog, who is usually aloof, jumps up on you and gives you kisses.

These seemingly random acts of affection could be a way for your deceased pet to let you know that they are still with you, watching over you, and sending their love.

It's important to keep an open mind and heart when it comes to signs of communication from our pets. These signs can come in unexpected ways, and it's up to us to recognize and acknowledge them.

If you're feeling unsure, take some time to reflect on your pet's personality and what they might do to communicate with you. Remember that their love is eternal and they will always be with you in spirit.

Signal 87

I understand that the loss of a pet can be a difficult and emotional experience. While we may no longer have our beloved pet with us physically, they can still communicate with us in subtle ways.

One such sign may be the sighting of a dried bone on the street. This seemingly random occurrence may actually hold a deep and meaningful message from our departed pet.

Seeing a dried bone on the street can be a powerful symbol of the cycle of life and death. It may serve as a reminder that our pets have passed on, but their memory and spirit lives on.

It may also represent the idea that life continues on after death, and that our pets are still with us in some form or another.

This sign may also hold a more personal meaning. Perhaps the bone resembles one that belonged to our pet, or it was found in a location that holds a special significance to us.

Whatever the case may be, the sighting of a dried bone can serve as a comforting reminder that our pets are still with us in some way, and that they are watching over us.

One example of this is when a friend of mine lost her beloved dog, who loved to play with bones. A few days after her passing, my friend found a dried bone on her front porch.

At first, she was saddened by the sight of it, but soon realized that it was a message from her dog. She felt a sense of comfort and peace knowing that her dog was still with her in spirit.

It's important to remember that signs from our pets can come in many forms, and it's up to us to be open and aware of them.

The sighting of a dried bone on the street may seem like a small and insignificant event, but it can hold a much deeper meaning for those who are open to it.

It's a reminder that our pets are still with us, even if we can't see them, and that they will always hold a special place in our hearts.

Signal 88

One possible sign that our pet is still with us in some way is the sudden sounds coming from their pet bowl.

When we hear these sounds, we may be tempted to dismiss them as simply the result of the wind or some other natural cause. But sometimes, these sounds can occur even on a calm day, or when there is no obvious explanation for them. In those moments, we may find ourselves wondering if our pet is trying to communicate with us through these sounds.

It's important to note that there may be other explanations for these sounds, such as a nearby animal or an issue with the bowl itself.

However, for those who believe in the idea of pet communication beyond the physical realm, these sounds can hold special meaning.

For example, a friend of mine lost her cat last

year, and she told me that she heard a distinct clinking sound coming from his empty food bowl in the days following his passing.

She described it as the sound he used to make when he would push his food around the bowl with his nose. To her, it was a clear sign that he was still with her in some way.

While these signs may not be scientific proof of continued pet presence, they can provide comfort and solace to those who are grieving.

It's important to trust our own intuition and beliefs when it comes to these signs, and to find meaning in them that brings us peace.

Signal 89

When we lose a beloved pet, we may yearn for any kind of connection with them, no matter how small. Often, signs from the spirit world can come in the form of small and subtle details that may go unnoticed by others.

One such detail is the sudden sound of a pet water dispenser, which can signal that our departed pet is trying to communicate with us.

These sounds can come in the form of a small trickle or splash, or even a larger gurgling noise. Whatever the sound, it can feel like a comforting reminder that our pet is still with us in some way.

We may feel a sense of relief, knowing that our pet is still watching over us and trying to let us know they are still here.

For me, one such experience occurred after the loss of my cat, who loved to drink from a water fountain. I had turned off the fountain and put it away, but one day, while sitting in my living room, I heard the sound of the fountain turning on and water flowing.

I went to investigate and found that the fountain was still unplugged and had not been touched.

While some might dismiss this as a coincidence or a technical malfunction, to me it felt like a sign from my beloved pet, letting me know that she was still around and looking out for me.

These small but meaningful signs can help us feel connected to our departed pets and provide us with a sense of comfort during a difficult time.

Signal 90

As someone who has lost a beloved pet, I know how difficult it can be to come to terms with their passing. However, there are times when we may receive signs from beyond that help to comfort us and reassure us that our pets are still with us in some way.

One such sign could be seeing a cartoon character that looks exactly like your pet. It may seem like a coincidence, but to me, it is a clear message that my pet is still with me in spirit.

The character may have similar markings or features, or even share the same personality traits as my pet did.

For example, I once saw a cartoon dog on a TV show that looked exactly like my late poodle. It had the same fur, distinctive markings on its face, and even the same mannerisms as my pet.

Seeing that dog on the screen made me feel

like my pet was sending me a message, letting me know that he was still with me in some way.

It's important to remember that these signs may not always be clear or obvious, but they can provide us with a sense of comfort and peace in our grieving process. By remaining open to the signs around us, we can find solace and a renewed connection to our beloved pets, even after they have passed on.

Signal 91

Seeing memories of your beloved pet on your Facebook feed can bring back a flood of emotions, both happy and sad. But what if those memories were more than just a reminder of the past? What if they were a sign that your pet is still with you, communicating in a way that only you can understand?

When we lose a pet, it's natural to cling to anything that reminds us of them. For many of us, social media has become a way to hold onto those memories and keep our pets close, even after they're gone.

But have you ever noticed that certain memories seem to pop up at just the right moment, when you need them the most? Maybe it's a photo of your pet cuddled up with you on a bad day, or a video of them doing something silly that always makes you laugh.

These memories may seem random, but they could be a sign that your pet is trying to reach out to you.

I remember one day, feeling particularly sad about the loss of my cat, I opened up my Facebook and the first thing I saw was a photo I had posted a year ago of my cat snuggling with me.

It was as if she was telling me she was still there, still with me, and that everything was going to be okay. In that moment, I felt a sense of peace and comfort that I hadn't felt since she passed away.

It's important to note that not everyone believes in signs from beyond, and that's okay. But if you do, and you find comfort in the idea that your pet is still with you, then trust in those moments when memories of your pet seem to come out of nowhere.

Trust that they are a sign that your pet is still communicating with you in their own special way. Trust that the love you shared with them is still alive and well, and that they will always be a part of your life.

In the end, it's up to us to interpret the signs

and symbols that we see, and to find our own meaning in them.

Whether it's a memory on Facebook, a bird singing outside your window, or a rainbow after a storm, these signs can bring us comfort and remind us that our pets are always with us in spirit.

Signal 92

Sometimes our pets find a way to break through that barrier and communicate with us through other people. For example, when someone unexpectedly brings up your pet in a conversation, it could be a sign that your pet is trying to communicate with you.

It's easy to dismiss these moments as coincidence, but when they happen repeatedly or in unexpected ways, it's worth considering if there is a deeper meaning behind them.

Perhaps a friend who has never mentioned your pet before suddenly tells you about a dream they had with your pet in it.

One personal example of this happened to me when I was going through a particularly difficult time after the loss of my dog. I was feeling very disconnected from the world around me, but one day a stranger in a coffee shop overheard me talking about my dog and came up to me to tell me how much they reminded her of her own beloved pet.

It was a small moment, but it felt like a powerful message from my dog, reminding me that I was not alone in my grief.

Of course, it's important not to read too much into every mention of our pets, as it can be a common topic of conversation for many people. But when it feels like more than just coincidence, it's worth considering the possibility that our pets are finding a way to communicate with us through the people around us.

Signal 93

One signal from pet heaven is the sudden appearance of a pet who just passed away and suffered the same death as our beloved pet.

It can be hard to understand why this would be a sign from our pets, but it can be seen as a way of our pets to communicate their continued presence with us.

It could also be seen as a way for us to find comfort in the fact that our pets are no longer suffering, and that they are now at peace.

This sign can be a reminder that our pets are still with us in spirit, and that they are still watching over us, even after they have passed.

For example, let's say your pet passed away due to a rare disease. A few weeks later, you hear about a pet who passed away from the same rare disease.

This sudden coincidence can feel like a

message from your pet, telling you that they are still here with you.

It could also provide comfort in knowing that you are not alone in your loss, and that there are others who understand what you are going through.

It's important to trust in these signs and take comfort in the fact that our pets continue to watch over us, even after they have passed on.

These signs can provide us with a sense of peace and healing during a difficult time, and help us to remember the joy and love that our pets brought into our lives.

Signal 94

When you lose a beloved pet, it can be difficult to let go of the memory of their presence. The sound of their name is ingrained in our memories, and it can be easy to call out to them without even realizing it.

However, there may be moments when calling out to them triggers an unexpected response, leading you to believe that your pet is communicating with you from beyond the veil.

It can be a startling experience when you catch yourself calling your pet's name out loud, only to realize they are no longer there.

But sometimes, in that moment of forgetfulness, you may hear or sense a subtle response, almost as if they are still present with you.

For instance, you may be going about your day when you suddenly hear yourself call out to your pet, saying "Here boy!" or "Come here, kitty!"

At that moment, you may sense an unusual stillness or feel a chill in the air, as if your pet is responding to your call. Or, you may hear a faint meow or bark, almost as if they are still with you.

It's important to remember that these experiences are personal and unique to each individual, and not everyone will believe in the idea of communication from beyond the grave.

However, if you do believe in the possibility of these signs, they can provide a sense of comfort and peace, knowing that your beloved pet is still with you in some way.

Ultimately, whether or not you believe in these signs, the love and connection we share with our pets never truly fades.

Their memory lives on in our hearts and in the little moments we share with them, even if it's just calling out their name from time to time.

Signal 95

The memories and experiences we shared with them are etched into our hearts and minds forever. These memories can sometimes lead to unexpected signs that our pets are still with us, even after they have passed away.

One such sign is feeling drawn to walk in the same place and at the same time that we used to walk our pet. This can be a powerful and emotional experience that can leave us feeling a sense of connection with our pet and a sense of comfort that they are still with us in some way.

When I lost my dog, I used to take him for a walk every morning in a nearby park.

After he passed away, I found myself drawn to that same park and would often walk there at the same time we used to walk together.

At first, it was difficult to walk in the same place and not have him by my side, but eventually, it became a way for me to feel close to him and remember the joy he brought to my life.

This sign that our pet is still with us can also be seen in the synchronicity of our actions.

For example, we may find ourselves waking up at the same time as we used to when we would take our pet out for a walk or feeling the urge to go on a walk at a specific time of day.

These moments can be a way for our pet to communicate with us, letting us know that they are still by our side and guiding us through life.

In conclusion, feeling drawn to walk in the same place and at the same time we used to walk our pet can be a powerful sign that our pet is still with us.

Signal 96

One of the ways that our pets may communicate with us after they've gone is through the things that remind us of them, like buying their favorite food at the store.

When I lost my pet, I found myself walking down the pet food aisle at the grocery store out of habit, even though I knew that I didn't need to buy food for them anymore.

But as I reached for their favorite brand, I felt a sense of comfort wash over me, as though my pet was still there with me, guiding me to make the right choice.

This feeling of comfort is not uncommon, and it's possible that our pets communicate with us through these small moments, reminding us of the joy and love they brought into our lives.

It's a reminder that even though they may not be physically present, our pets are still with us in spirit.

Other examples of this could include finding their favorite toy or blanket in the back of a closet or seeing a brand of treats that you always used to give them.

These small moments can be bittersweet, but they can also bring a sense of peace and comfort knowing that our pets are still with us in some way.

It's important to remember that grief is a process, and it's okay to feel a range of emotions as we navigate the loss of a pet.

But when we experience these small reminders, it can help us feel a sense of connection to our pets, and remind us of the joy they brought into our lives.

Signal 97

Even the most mundane tasks, such as scheduling a grooming appointment, can suddenly bring up memories and emotions.

It can be difficult to accept that our pets are no longer with us, but sometimes they find ways to remind us that they are still with us in spirit.

One such way is when we receive reminders for appointments that were scheduled for our pets before they passed away. It can be a jarring experience to see your pet's name on an appointment reminder, especially if it's been some time since they passed away.

But rather than feeling sad or overwhelmed, we can choose to see it as a sign that our pet is still watching over us.

Perhaps your pet had a regular grooming schedule and you receive a reminder for their next appointment. Or maybe you get a reminder for a vet checkup or vaccination that your pet would normally have had around this time of year.

These reminders can be bittersweet, but they can also be a reminder of the love and care we gave our pets while they were with us.

In my own experience, I've received reminders for my cat's annual checkup long after she passed away. Each time it happened, it brought up memories of taking her to the vet and the little rituals we had around the experience.

It was a reminder of the love I had for her and the love she had for me.

So if you find yourself receiving reminders for your pet's appointments, try to see it as a sign that your pet is still with you.

Use it as an opportunity to reflect on the memories you shared and the love you still have for them. It may not make the pain of their loss go away, but it can bring a sense of comfort and peace.

Signal 98

Cleaning up after many years can be a daunting task, both physically and emotionally.

While sorting through old paperwork and files, one may come across various documents related to their deceased pet, such as lab tests, appointments, and medical bills.

At first, it may feel overwhelming and difficult to process, but it can also be a sign that your pet is communicating with you from beyond the veil.

These physical reminders of our pets can evoke powerful emotions and serve as a tangible connection to their memory. It can be a bittersweet experience to go through these documents, as it brings back memories of the moments we shared with our beloved pets.

In my own experience, I recently came across old vet bills from my cat's final months, and it brought up a lot of emotions for me. It was a reminder of the love and care that went into taking care of her, but also the pain of having to say goodbye.

However, in that moment, I felt a sense of peace knowing that my cat was still communicating with me in her own way, reminding me of the love and joy we shared together.

These documents can also serve as a reminder to cherish the time we have with our furry friends while they are still with us. It's important to take the opportunity to make memories and enjoy every moment we have together.

In the end, finding these documents can be a powerful sign that our pets are still with us in spirit and continue to communicate with us in subtle ways.

It's up to us to remain open and receptive to these messages, and to treasure the memories we have shared with our beloved companions.

Signal 99

Hearing a song with your pet's name can be a powerful reminder of their presence, even though they're no longer physically here.

In those moments, it's as if the universe is conspiring to remind us of our beloved furry friend. The lyrics and melody can evoke strong emotions, triggering memories of the times we spent together and the love we shared.

I remember when I lost my dog, I would often hear a particular song on the radio that had his name in the chorus. At first, it was difficult to hear, as it brought up painful emotions.

But as time went on, I started to find comfort in the fact that it was like he was saying hello from the other side.

The song became a sort of anthem for our time together, and hearing it felt like a special moment of connection with him.

It was like he was still present in my life in some small way, guiding me through the difficult days without him.

In those moments, I found myself feeling grateful for the time we had together and the love that we shared.

Hearing his name in a song reminded me that even though he was gone, the memories and the love we shared would always be a part of me.

So, if you find yourself hearing a song with your pet's name, allow yourself to feel the emotions that come up.

Take it as a sign that your furry friend is still with you, watching over you and reminding you of the love that you shared.

Signal 100

When we go through a significant loss, like the death of a beloved pet, it is common to associate specific songs or sounds with that loss.

It could be a song that played during a special moment shared with the pet, or one that we listened to during their last moments.

Either way, when we hear that song unexpectedly, it can feel like our pet is trying to communicate with us, reminding us of their presence and the memories we shared.

I understand how emotional and powerful this experience can be. It can be a mix of nostalgia, sadness, and even joy as we remember the good times we had with our furry friends.

One time I was feeling really down about the passing of my cat and I heard a song that I used to play when we were cuddling, and it felt like she was still there with me. It was like she was saying,

"I'm still here, I'm still with you."

These signs can be a source of comfort, reminding us that our pets' spirits live on in our memories and hearts. It's okay to feel emotional when we experience them, and it's okay to take time to reflect on what they mean to us.

It can be a beautiful way to connect with our pets even after they have passed.

Remember that everyone's experience with grief is unique, and the way we process it can be different. These signs are not a guarantee, but they can bring some solace and help us cope with the pain.

Signal 101

When we lose a beloved pet, the pain and grief can be overwhelming. We may find ourselves struggling to cope with the sudden absence of our furry friend, and it's natural to want to find some way to connect with them, even if they're no longer with us.

One way that our pets may communicate with us after they've passed is by giving us a sudden urge to talk to them.

This can happen when we're feeling particularly down or overwhelmed, or even when we're just going about our daily routine.

We may suddenly feel the need to share our thoughts and feelings with our lost pet, to seek their comfort and support. It's as if we can feel their presence with us, even though they're no longer physically here.

When this happens, it's important to

remember that our pets are always with us in spirit.

They may not be able to respond in the same way they did in life, but they can still hear us and feel our love. It can be helpful to talk to our pets in these moments, to share our feelings and let them know how much we miss them.

Examples of this could be when you're having a particularly hard day at work, and suddenly find yourself wishing your pet was there to comfort you.

Or when you're out on a walk and feel a sudden urge to talk to your pet about what you're seeing or feeling.

It could even happen when you're at home, going about your daily routine, and suddenly find yourself drawn to a place where you used to spend time with your pet.

Whatever the circumstances, it's important to allow yourself to feel the emotions and to reach out to your pet in whatever way feels most comfortable to you.

Your pet may not be able to respond in the same way they did in life, but they can still bring comfort and peace to your heart.

A Message From Pet Heaven

My dearest human,

I know that you are grieving and that it
feels like you will never find peace.

But please remember that I am with you always,
watching over you and sending you all of my love.

I am grateful for the time we spent
together, for the laughter and the joy
and the bond that we shared.

Please don't blame yourself for anything.

You did everything you could to take
care of me, and I know that you loved me
more than anything in the world.

It was just my time to go, and even though it
hurts, we both know that it was the right thing.

I want you to know that I am at peace

now, and that I am no longer in pain.

I am running through fields of flowers, chasing butterflies, and basking in the sunshine.

And even though we are no longer together in body, we will always be together in spirit.

Thank you for being the best human a pet could ever ask for.

You gave me a life full of love, and I will cherish every moment we spent together forever.

All my love,

Your cutest and most beloved pet

Mindfulness and Meditation

I hope that 101 Signals From Pet Heaven help you deal with the loss of your best friend. Mindfulness and Meditation help a lot when it comes to healing all areas of your life.

Unlock the secrets to a more Fulfilling Life with the Power of Mindfulness and Manifestation.

Mindful Manifestor - Achieving Mindfulness for Effective Manifestations is your ultimate guide to realizing your Full Potential, Bringing your Dreams to Life, and Finding Peace of Mind.

You'll learn how to:

- Quiet your inner voice
- Align your Thoughts and Emotions with your Desires and
- Find the Peace of mind that comes with Living a Life of Purpose and Abundance

Whether you're new to the concept or have been manifesting for some time, this book provides a Fresh Perspective and Actionable Steps to Elevate your Manifestation practice.

Read Here

Free Manifestation Journal

JUPITERION
www.jupiterion.com

I want to invite you to my VIP newsletter.

IT DOESN'T COST ANYTHING. All you have to do is Join my Mailing List.

I will be sending you FREE Exclusive Content that you won't find anywhere else.

Here is My First Gift

I'll also be sending you Announcements regarding my Promos and New Books. I will not send you anything that's not related to my content.

CLICK TO DOWNLOAD
JOURNAL

Or Copy this Link -> https://stats.sender.net/forms/elL85e/view

Note: Please check your Spam or Promotions tab

if the confirmation doesn't arrive in your inbox.

Enjoy,

Jupiterion Olympus

Author's Message

Thank you so much for reading *101 Signals From Pet Heaven – Signs your Beloved Pet Thinks of You in the Afterlife.* If you found this book helpful, feel free to check my other guides out by searching for Jupiterion Olympus.

Also check these out for the latest news about my books.

Website – http://www.jupiterion.wordpress.com

Mailing List - https://stats.sender.net/forms/elL85e/view